Mark

Share the book
if you like it!

Lali

RELENTLESS BRUSH STROKES
A Memoir

Lalitha Shankar

AuthorHouse™
1663 Liberty Drive, Suite 200
Bloomington, IN 47403
www.authorhouse.com
Phone: 1-800-839-8640

© 2008 Lalitha Shankar. All rights reserved.

No part of this book may be reproduced, stored in a retrieval system, or transmitted by any means without the written permission of the author.

First published by AuthorHouse   10/7/2008

ISBN: 978-1-4343-5803-5 (sc)

Printed in the United States of America
Bloomington, Indiana

This book is printed on acid-free paper.

Front cover
(Pilgrims waiting in a queue to enter a temple
Painting by Mr. P. Rangaswamy)
Photography
By
Dr. Jitender Sehgal

PROLOGUE

This memoir is one daughter's version of her father. If a man had ten children and the children each had to relate a story about their father, there would be ten different amusing and interesting stories. Moreover, it is hard to just write one daughter's viewpoint without muddying it with recollections of other people, who were deeply interwoven into the life's canvas painted by her father. I tried to be nonjudgmental and at the same time take everything that happened in a light vein. For all those who do not know Appa, read along and get a flavor of an interesting man. For those who know him, relive the moments that you have spent with him.

Many who have been important in his life have been excluded, and many who played minor roles in his interesting life have been portrayed to showcase Appa's canvas. After all, one's gaze should be directed to the small stones beneath the tree, even though it is the tree that is the subject in the painting. I apologize to all those who have not been mentioned in this book.

A friend once said, "If a man is a hero in his home, how does it matter what I think of him?" This holds true for all. Appa was a "hero in his home." *Relentless Brushstrokes* is the introduction of this man to the world. His Technicolor world and life continues to amaze all his family members. Some were surprised that he was able to have a long married life, while others questioned his carefree attitudes. Was he a victim of his father's domineering personality, or was he a fabrication of his own faults? While all those who knew him continued to analyze his character, he had unbiased admirers in his three children.

My sister Swathi once waved to a painting created by her father that was moving on the wall from a gust of wind. When asked why she waved to a lifeless painting, she commented, "I said hi to Appa, as I felt his presence in the wind that shook his painting."

Appa is alive in his painting. If only I could write Appa's name on a grain of sand, I may have tried it to please him. But he has immortalized himself in the few paintings that decorate our homes.

If you have not expressed your feelings to your parents who are still alive, please do so before it is too late. Or else you will have the burden and/or the pleasure to express all of your feelings that you had not articulated to them when they were with you.

This is the cross that I carry. I wish that I had been more supportive of Appa and expressed my love. "Better late than never" is the path taken by my culpable self in my memoir.

DEDICATED

To the memory of my father, P. Rangaswamy
And
For my mother, who continues to be the force behind me.

Table of Contents

CHAPTER 1
The Birth of Ambi the Artist 5

CHAPTER 2
Growing Between Reality Checks and Films 17

CHAPTER 3
Dad Meets Mom 33

CHAPTER 4
Wedding Day 47

CHAPTER 5
And Then There Were Three 59

CHAPTER 6
Thatha's Telegram 75

CHAPTER 7
Madras Express with Mom 81

CHAPTER 8
Chitthappa's Wedding 91

CHAPTER 9
King of Cricket 103

CHAPTER 10
Veshti with Vengeance 117

CHAPTER 11
Artist Dad 127

CHAPTER 12
A Parent Apparent 139

CHAPTER 13
　　Literary Lot 149

CHAPTER 14
　　Mantras and Vedas 157

CHAPTER 15
　　Arranged Marriages by Swamy 165

CHAPTER 16
　　Father's Famous Festival 177

CHAPTER 17
　　Clairvoyance 191

CHAPTER 18
　　Classical Appa 203

CHAPTER 19
　　At the Movies with Appa 211

CHAPTER 20
　　Appa Meets His Son 223

CHAPTER 21
　　End of Thatha's Era 229

CHAPTER 22
　　The Fatal Fracture 233

CHAPTER 23
　　Recovering from Surgery 239

CHAPTER 24
　　Appa's Memories Are Alive 261

GLOSSARY OF TERMS 267

CHAPTER 1

> "If for a tranquil mind you seek
> These things observe with care
> Of whom you speak, to whom you speak
> And how, and when and where."
>
> Anonymous author

I have climbed up and down the same stairs many times for many years. I do not pay attention to the 5 × 3 feet painting of the trees portraying change of color in the autumn season. It has been hanging in the same spot for the last twenty-two years. How many of us stop and stare at our wall hangings every day? It is only the new ones that we hang that receive a special spotlight, up until such time that they also become just other old pictures on another wall. *The Autumn Touch* is just another decoration on the wall. The painting is large and has snuggled comfortably at the top of the stairs for all to view. The only time I pay any notice to it is when someone new walks into our home and asks me, "Who did that painting? It's beautiful."

"My father painted that piece," I immediately gloat in reply.

It is another one of those Sunday mornings. I am slowly making my way downstairs. Instead of quickly running down the stairs impatiently for my morning cup of coffee, I stop to look at the painted tree and the brushstrokes and thick paint that have been layered over its bark. I can remember my father's small, frail frame bent over the canvas creating every splash of color, and the light and shadows he deftly brushed on to bring life to the branches and the fallen leaves. I have this urge to stand and stare a little longer at the painting. For some reason, this day I am almost in tune with my psyche, and the cosmic forces have me focused on the tree. I can almost see my father, Appa, peering at me from behind it. *I cannot ignore him.* Is it just my imagination playing games? He deserves more than just a passing glance. So, I stop to look at Appa. He looks happy and content and is as usual curious to see if I am happy and content. He beckons me and I catch a glimpse of his tobacco tucked on the side of his mouth as he gives me a half smile. Is he trying to tell me something from behind the tree? Or am I just imagining all this? Is he asking me to come and take a stroll with him down the lane that he has created in his painting?

I allow my curiosity to hold me captive in front of a painting that had been long forgotten. Appa, I think I will walk with you. I want to see where you are. Shall this be the first beer we share while ruminating about bygone days?

Am I crazy? Or am I finally getting in touch with the chakras of my inner conscience that will enable me to visualize Appa? Will I get in touch with him in a celestial way and ruminate over the time we spent together? Let me meditate. We take a seat under the amber-stained canopy.

The Birth of Ambi the Artist

> He wants to live on through something—
> and in his case, his masterpiece is his son.
> All of us want that, and it gets poignant as
> we get more anonymous in this world.
> —Arthur Miller

A beautiful day had dawned in Madras. My grandmother, Patti, gave birth to a beautiful baby boy. The timing could not have been better. My grandfather, Thatha, a slowly rising film producer and director, believed that he owed his change of luck and good fortunes to this handsome baby, a truly wonderful gift from God. Their firstborn child was their lucky star that was shining bright and strong. The *puniyav janam* (auspicious birth), a grand celebration on the tenth day to name their son, took place at their lovely home. The child was named after his grandfather and nicknamed Ambi. For five years they longed and yearned for a child, and they were finally rewarded with a lovely baby. This child, their fortune, had resulted and was beyond blissful. Thatha proved to be a proud father to his firstborn son.

Ambi enlightened Thatha's and Patti's lives and grew up in a household with a silver spoon in his mouth. He was a curious, healthy, and active child. His mother spent a large part of her day devoted to taking care of him, as he could easily get into trouble with his curiosity. Ambi was not alone for long. His brothers and sisters joined him in the household, which kept Thatha's and Patti's lives eventful and hectic.

Patti, who was always up by 4:30 a.m., spent a large part of the day in the kitchen, a simple large room. It had a window at one end with a sink below it. To the right of the sink was a counter with a stove. There was one wall lined with cupboards for storage, and we always sat on the floor. Thatha had a plank made of rosewood, a popular seat in those days. The dining room with the fridge also served as the room where the religious activities took place. The kitchen was always clean, and servants were not allowed into the kitchen for religious reasons. Patti started the day by boiling water to make fresh coffee percolated through the South Indian coffee filter. She had this coffee grinder which ground the exact amount of the roasted beans. This was packed tightly in the bottom of the filter, and boiling hot water was poured into it. As the aroma of coffee would infiltrate the air,

Thatha would walk into the kitchen for his fresh morning cup of coffee, which was served in his tall, stainless steel glass. Thatha began his day after *Sandhyavandanam,* his morning prayers.

Thatha and Patti may have been influential and wealthy, but they lived a simple and humble life. This humility was seen in Appa, my father, and in all of my uncles and aunts. The brothers and sisters shared bedrooms, and Appa's bedroom was in the top floor directly above Thatha's office. It had a lot of windows, and was bright and small. It looked over the front yard and opened onto a large balcony. As the room was small, no one shared it with him.

Thatha and Patti's home had seven children. The younger ones did not have to worry about getting up early, but there were college students and schoolgoers who had to be up. When Appa was twenty-two years of age, his youngest sister was just born. Patti patiently carried out her motherly duties toward all of her children painstakingly. She single-handedly manipulated everyone out of the house every morning. This was not an easy feat when she had to get their lunches ready too. She, like many women of her era, did not take her job in the kitchen lightly, and she did not give up that job to a cook easily. No cooks could survive under her vigilance and analysis. So, guess who was the boss of the kitchen?

"Where are your children? Don't they have to go to school? Wake them up before it's too late," Thatha said.

"Let them sleep in. They had a hard day. Between homework, cricket games, and drama practices, they're all exhausted. School is not like when you attended. These children are expected to perform like circus monkeys," she told him.

"Why don't you say their school is not like the one you went to?" Thatha teased Patti.

Patti schooled up to fifth grade. If she had received a university education, India's face may have changed long before it got its independence from the British. She was a woman with a vision, and her knowledge about nature, natural therapy, healthy meals, and environmentally friendly formulas that ranged from household goods to hair growth was awe inspiring. She knew the right therapy even for her ailing cows. She was Julia Child, Anita Roddick, and Martha Stewart all rolled into one. The only person missing in her life was a promotional manager for all her talents, who could have made her a living legend. She lives in all of our hearts as one of the most important people who honed Appa's life. She laid the frame for the canvas of Appa's picturesque life.

On the days that Thatha had to get ready for film shooting early in the morning, Patti would run in circles around him to make sure that he was on time. His assistants started arriving in the morning, and some days work had already begun at the doorstep of Ambi's home.

As a child, I always remember that my grandfather's home was an abode that never rested. Early in the morning, Gopal the milkman tended to the cows and milked them. He knocked on the back door and brought in the fresh warm milk. I can still visualize him in his white cotton wrap around his waist, a *veshti,* a checkered shirt, and a towel tied around his head.

Thatha's home was a large mansion. The activity in the morning was in the back of the home. A large room opened into the kitchen on one side, and another doorway led into the back garden from a small back foyer which had steps to the back garden. The back garden had a large concrete patio, beyond which was an outhouse to the left and a well which provided fresh water. Past the outhouse was a large garden. A garden path led to the cow stall, which was to one side of the patio, with the car garage on the other. The garden had mango trees, coconut trees, and chickoo trees. Patti was an avid gardener and tended to a large vegetable patch on the side of the outhouse.

The most enthusiastic person at 4 a.m. in the morning was Patti. A petite and beautiful woman in nine yards of a sari, all wrapped to her small frame, she descended the stairs and welcomed Gopal with a smile. The one person other than her family who brought smile to her face was Gopal.

"Gopal, there is very little milk in the cylinder."

"Amma, I don't know what happened to Raji. Today I'll take her to the vet."

"Is it only Raji that is not okay? You're not feeding the cows well. Could you please make sure that the fodder has added nourishments?" she suggested.

I remember some of the conversations. If she thought that the cows were not doing well, she would go up to the cows and give them pep talks. If there were no bananas for breakfast or any left over from last night's dinner, these items had already reached one of the four stomachs of her precious cows.

"Your grandmother nursed the cows before she nursed us all," Appa's younger brother, Balram Chitthappa, who had a great sense of humor, commented if he saw no bananas for breakfast in the morning.

"At least you humans ask for what you want and you get it. What about these poor animals that do not speak and express? They could starve if we do not feed them," retorted Patti.

"Your children may go hungry, Amma, but not your cows," he replied jokingly.

Chitthappa was the jovial, easygoing man in Thatha and Patti's household. He always had a sunny way of delivering his jokes about the daily happenings in the household.

I did spend a lot of time with Thatha and Patti in the kitchen listening in on their conversations. As a child, I was always curious about Appa and had many questions about him for Patti.

"Patti, did Appa look like me when he was a little boy?" I inquired. "Everybody tells me that I resemble him."

"You don't bear any resemblance to him. He has sharp features; big, large, expressive eyes that can be compared to a split mango; and his lips are as if they were etched on a statue by immortal hands," replied Patti proudly, describing Appa's good looks.

"Patti, about the statue part, you're correct. I think God created Appa from the Deccan granite stone and left him too long to bake in the kiln," I replied jokingly as I commented on Appa's looks. She was serious about Appa's good looks and ignored my teasing comment on Appa's rich tan. Color was not something we gave any importance to in my grandparents' home. South Indians for that matter were every shade of imaginable browns, and the North Indians had a lighter hue. Yellow, rose, and peach hues mixed with the burnt sienna and maddock brown is probably what one would mix to get the appropriate colors to paint an Indian. On the other hand, God's palette for the Southern Indians lacked the yellows, rose, and the peach hues.

Generally speaking, the South Indians are the true Dravidian clans. The North Indians had their lives changed over 1000 years by intermarriages and have a lighter and a better complexion—*according to them.* Indians love to discuss the color of the skin, but we do not like to call ourselves racists, as we have fallen prey to racism in our own land. This is largely due to our eagerness to migrate in search of work. The discrimination we experience within India is mostly from religious differences and the divisions brought on by class, profession, and, of course, colors.

This story is not about India. It is about my dear *appa,* who tastefully changed the way I look at this world. The only colors I knew were the colors he mixed on a palette before he started a painting. He mixed colors like I have known no living person to do. Appa's passion with paint could be seen in his generous play with the primary colors on the palette. His next step was to use palette knives and mix in various amounts of white, raw umber, and burnt sienna and bring about the right shade, tone, and hue before he took it to the canvas. He was well known for directly applying all colors without blending onto the canvas, and the brushstrokes and play of light made the difference to the painting. He always spoke about the colors as fiery, warm, bright, or subdued depending upon the mood he wanted to depict in his painting. When he had the paintbrush in his hands, he entered a different stratosphere, where we could see, sense, and appreciate only his own aesthetics. We were in the next orbit revolving around his beautiful life that he created for all to see and experience.

"Don't be naughty. Your dad looked like Lord Krishna," Patti said. I was correct about the dark chiseled stone and the treatment it received in the kiln. "He was so charming, with an enchanting smile," she continued. When she looked at my dad, Patti saw the entire universe in his eyes, just like Yeshodha saw the universe in her son when Lord Krishna opened his mouth. "I always dressed him in white or cream-colored *jubbas*," she continued. A *jubba* is a light muslin cloth loosely made into a vest for a baby's comfort. I can confirm that these are the most comfortable outfits for children born in hot tropical climates.

"Patti, was he good at school? Did he come first, like I do sometimes?"

"What do you think? Where did you think you got your brains? If you sow an apple tree, you don't reap a weed," she boasted. She forgot my mother's contribution for this permutation. "He was always first. But, he was a little playful. Boys are always boys. He was a handful, but I would not have traded him for anybody else," she said with a smile.

Hearing our discussion about Appa's childhood and youth, Thatha walked into the kitchen for some more coffee. "Who are you discussing?" he inquired.

"Appa," I replied proudly.

"What is his mother telling you about his childhood?" he asked.

"Patti is telling me about how he was talented and he painted so well."

"Is she telling you about how he played truant and how he got into a lot of trouble at school by not being attentive?" he challenged.

"She's only a child and wanted to know about how good-looking her father was and so on," Patti said protectively. "Please don't belittle her father. She has to respect him, and you shouldn't pass disparaging remarks about him."

These reactions from Patti when Thatha intervened did not mean much when I was young. But, as I grew up, I realized that Patti was the Rock of Gibraltar for Appa. He hid behind her sari, especially when he knew he was not right. Appa always counted on her for any bad blotches that he created on his life painting. She offered him techniques to hide the flaws made on his canvas. She changed his palette and handed him paint thinners when she knew that the colors were too harsh and might cause a scene when his father arrived.

Thus, my dad began life's illustrious art lessons holding on to his mother's styled brushes. Always looking up to his father for some approval or appreciation, and fearful of rejection of any of his creations or endeavors by his father, Appa was in limbo whenever he crafted his life's portrait. Although I did not look at Thatha the way my father projected him to me, I could see that grandparents were tough when bringing up their own children and softened when they dealt with their grandchildren. I could see that when my grandparents dealt with us and when my parents dealt with their grandchildren too. Love's tender brushes were used as grandparents.

Thatha was the disciplinarian who held a stick in his hand and not only waved it. Wonderful things happened in his life, but he did not spare corporal punishment. A successful businessman, domineering and demanding, Thatha held only metaphoric pencils in his hands. He did not believe in erasers. How do you draw your road to destiny without using the erasers to occasionally clear the rough rocks from the pavement?

Appa, a free spirit, did accept his father's pencils, and under the disapproving eyes of his father he continued to texture; he shaded his life without the help of an eraser. The fine faults he committed were hidden behind the thick colorful brushstrokes that he chose to cover over the preliminary sketches of his life. He created his colorful life on the big, blank, symbolic canvas laid down by his parents. The colors and exclusive brushstrokes he used were masterful and unique.

A father dreams for his son, and sure enough my grandfather dreamt all that he could for my father. But it was Thatha's dream and not Appa's. Appa had his own dreams and nightmares. He visualized and conceptualized those that he wished. Appa continued to do what pleased him.

Was Appa a realist, expressionist, or an impressionist? When it came to his life, I leave it for all to decide. His life he painted skillfully with brushes handed to him by his parents and his wife, drawing upon the habits that he'd acquired during his life. As the English would say, you make your bed and you sleep on it.

"Appa, who do you think you resemble most when you look at the lives of many great artists?" I asked.

"I think I am a combination of many. As we say in our Hindu religion, these artists from all over the world are ubiquitous in all created beings. I for one sometimes emulate Van Gogh in his restlessness, impatience, and short-tempered moodiness. He had his brother Theo to support him, and I have your mother. There are days my life sounds like Claude Monet, who had issues with his father—like I do."

Appa never blamed Thatha for anything. He may not have agreed with his father, but never did he disrespect him. Appa was solely responsible for his and his family's destiny, and on that Thatha would second me.

CHAPTER 2
Growing Between Reality Checks and Films

> It is a wise father that knows his own child.
> —William Shakespeare

Thatha and Patti had a beautiful, palatial home. It was in the heart of the city, with a beautiful garden and a front gate with a steel archway designed by Appa. This archway was completely covered by a thick vine of magenta bougainvilleas. The walls of the garden had oleander and frangipani flower bushes. The prettiest tree was a tall, majestic Ashoka that had been planted by Appa. This tree was graceful, with beautiful foliage, and it bore lovely orange flowers. A poplar tree variety, it plays a significant role from a religious and historical standpoint, as Lord Buddha was supposed to have been born under the shades of this majestic tree. It gave character to the beautiful home. A large open verandah had a few steps that led into the front yard.

Thatha and Patti had a growing family. By the time my dad was ten years old, he had three brothers and a sister. With Thatha's busy work schedule, the onus of bringing up the family was left to the loving and caring Patti. Thatha had made a few successful silent movies, and by 1929, when my father was six years old, he had made a successful talking film. A pioneer in the Indian film industry, he was often traveling or in the studio shooting movies. Thatha made many more movies, and along with his friend went on to set up the very first film studio, Associated Madras Film Studio, in Saidapet. In the days when talkie movies and silent movies were screened for the British, Madras was well known for its cinemas. Tents were set up in various parts of the city where movie buffs would buy tickets to sit on the floor or on chairs to enjoy these black-and-white films.

It must have been a lot of fun. The tickets cost a lot less if one sat on the hard floor as opposed to the chairs. These tents were temporarily erected; a town crier would announce to the local community about the upcoming event, and you could buy your tickets in advance. My mother and her grandmother went to one of these movies. The excitement about seeing a movie and the unbearable heat within the tent lolled my mother to sleep, and she does not remember the movie at all. But, she does remember her grandmother being all emotional over the story line and weeping throughout the movie.

When these movie theatres became permanent structures, the extra piece of luxury were the ceiling fans. You have to live in a hot climate to understand one fact about fans. They just move the hot air from one hot corner of the room to another and do nothing to cool one off. Our family and my cousins' family were out at one of these theatres cooled by ceiling fans. We were thrilled to go to this matinee. Lo and behold, all of the fans except the one over our seats were functioning. We children were willing to put up with the heat so long as we could see the movie. Well, it was not meant to be. My mother's sister's husband, Periappa, a man with a lot of principle, got a refund from the management and returned home with seven inconsolable and disappointed children.

Appa was the biggest movie buff of us all. He may have skipped school to enjoy an afternoon at the movies. Appa had an equal number of friends and enemies and would invariably get caught red-handed. I was never surprised when I heard these stories. With Thatha for a father, I did not know how Appa dared such feats and expected to survive. Thatha may have made films, but it was not for the family's viewing pleasure. The movies were treated like forbidden delicious fruits at Thatha's place. His children and all those who married into this family were wary about openly appreciating or going to the movies. It was after he retired that it was easy for him to discuss his life as a movie producer and director.

Many afternoons we grandchildren would curl up with Thatha and he would reminisce about his life in films. The stories would keep us all entertained for hours. He enjoyed discussing the stories that he had written and spoke about some of the flops that he had created.

Thatha did not take Patti to movies because he did not believe in women going to them. He was not about to let his children have any growing interest in this field either. He felt lucky to have succeeded in it, but there was no guarantee that his sons would. This was Thatha's biased judgment and intuitive perception for his brood. Who was to question his parental authority or challenge what he deemed was appropriate? His reaction to movies probably reflected the Indian civilization and society of the early twentieth century. The Brahmins were interested but inhibited by their tradition-bound families from venturing into filmmaking as a profession. I cannot imagine what my grandfather must have gone through to take on a career that must have been frowned upon. This was probably the basis of Thatha's aversion toward Appa's interest in art and painting.

After all, Appa was interested in the still version of the art form that his father was fostering and making a living from. Why it was that Thatha did not want Appa to pursue a career in an art field is still a mystery to me. I have heard Thatha complain about how difficult it was to get reputable men and women to act in his movies. Early on, men would dress as women and play the female roles in Indian movies and theatre shows. It was not considered a decent profession, and an actress stood to be shunned for life. He did not think my dad was cut out to be in the arts. Besides, what would my father do in films anyway?—dress as a woman or paint still-life pictures and landscapes? Thatha didn't think that Appa was interested in the business end of filmmaking. Painting and art appreciation were not pastimes that Appa could enjoy at Thatha's place, as he was not encouraged, for fear that he might decide to deviate from choosing a conventional profession.

Patti, on the other hand, was proud to see her talented son paint. She would encourage him up to a point. She was also lenient and did not believe in any autocratic rules for the children. Appa and his siblings were all comfortable to come to her if they goofed or had any problems at school or with friends. She let them enjoy themselves and really believed that all work and no play were not good for the soul.

"You will all get caught today, and your dad is not going to be very pleased," Patti told Appa and his brothers. The new theatre had opened with a premiere showing of Alfred Hitchcock's *Rebecca*. Appa's favorite actor, Laurence Olivier, was in the movie, and he and his brothers decided to go for it. Of course, they were not about to take their sister. Who in their right mind wants to take their sister out with them?—and to an English movie at the large theatre? They had their mother to protect them from their dad's ire. Their sister knew nothing about this, and the brothers took off before their dad could return from work.

"Where are your sons?" Thatha inquired when he got home.

"Oh, they're visiting with their friends," Patti said evasively. She was partly correct. They *were* visiting with their friends, at the local theatre—a minor detail which their dad does not need to know about, especially after a trying day that he may have had at work. When they returned from the movies, Patti would let them in through the back door and quietly send them upstairs to their bed. She was there for them, but if they were caught in the act of returning from the movies, Thatha would chastise all, including Patti for being so devious and underhanded.

"You find thieves in a policeman's home. Well, you will find keen moviegoers in a grouchy filmmaker's home," my dad would retort if they were caught red-handed. Good for you, dad! Never would he dare to say this loud enough to his father. He never stood up to his father or questioned his authority. Thatha, who was a pragmatist and an idealist, presented Appa opportunities that were not conducive to Appa's imagination. Nevertheless, he was not about to question his father. He did what his father asked of him.

Ambi went to medical school and hated it. After wasting three years, empty-handed of a diploma or degree, he came back to face his father. He knew that he had disappointed his father in many ways. But, he did not know how to get out of this bad decision to become a doctor. "I will not go back," he told his parents. "I hate dissecting dead bodies. I don't enjoy reading and studying about diseases. Most of all, it's a field for people who want to commit to memory." He did not like memorizing and did not enjoy dissection.

"So, what are you going to do with your life?" Thatha angrily glared at Ambi. "Three years down the drain! You have nothing to show for them. You can't laze around in the house. I won't pay you a penny for your truancy."

"I'll do some other degree course, but I'm not going back to that depressing medical school," Ambi insisted.

It must have been a pretty bad scene that day. Thatha's opinion was that Ambi was lazy, not committed to a professional pursuit, and wasteful of money. My grandmother was so protective of her son's decision that she stood up for him.

"Do you want your son to venture out as a doctor who is incompetent, or do you want him to be good at what he wants to do?" Patti questioned Thatha. Ambi somehow escaped the wrath of his father and very quickly headed for another try at another career. This time he came back with degrees in chemistry, agriculture, and engineering.

Ambi was not suited for medicine. Now that I am a physician, I often wonder if Appa had attention deficit disorder (ADD), or whether all geniuses suffer from ADD. If he did, I am glad he was born in an era when Ritalin was not available. This would have destroyed all of his creativity, intelligence, and curiosity. These are the very three character traits in him which made him unique, exasperating, and fascinating.

Obedient Ambi did his best to hold on to his engineering profession while pining over painting being his passion. Patti had taken this to a different level. She would tell him to put away his canvas, as an evil eye might be cast on his great talents. What good was his great talent if he was not allowed to paint, and when he did he couldn't display his work?

You cannot stop a sun from rising; and in the same way, my dad could not be stopped. Patti had all her religious idols made by my dad for her during the festival season. This would just bring out the best in him. He would be called upon to do the decorations for the Navarathri festival, and for nine nights the entire neighborhood would be awestruck by his work. He continued to paint and give away his artwork to friends. His sisters were artists too. Patti was quite correct about her statement: You plant an apple seed and you will get apples. Thatha the artist, who preferred pursuing art in the film form, had created children just like himself.

My dad never asked us to pursue careers that he deemed correct for us. He had learned his lesson from his father. He gave us paint and the canvas and told us to depict what we thought was best for us. But when my dad was growing up, a father's word was like gospel, and he would not sway from it. He did what was right as a son, and Thatha did what was considered to be a father's job—molding his son to make him into a man who could bring home four square meals to his family. "Art does not bring money. Nobody collects a living artist's work in India." Thatha argued with Appa. This he was very right about. If Appa had continued with his art career and with his business acumen in selling his artwork, my mother would have had more challenges than she already had.

We can name a few artists who made a living from selling their artwork. Maqbool Hussain was born a decade before Appa and made it as an artist. Dad did not make that list. One time, a friend of his came over to our place. This was a long-lost friend who should have stayed lost. My mother did not like him and told my father to keep away from him.

But the friend returned the very next day with a proposal for my father. "Ambi, you're so talented. I'm sure I can help you by selling some of your paintings. I have friends in high places, and they're interested in collecting art. You can make a pretty penny from this, I can assure you."

Amma took Appa aside and warned him about this cheat who had come posing as an art dealer. "You stand to lose all the work that you have done to this man. Somehow he doesn't look me in my eye, and I don't trust people who avoid eye contact," said my mother. My mother was a strong believer that if two humans can see into each other's eyes, then they will not deceive each other. Fraudulent characters evade eye contact. Now if you see me stare and try looking into a person's eye, you know why. I fear being dismissed as a deceitful person!

To make a long story short, Appa gave this man all of the paintings that were decorating our home. We even helped load this man's car with the loot. We never heard from him again. Appa called his other friends and family members to find this thief's address or phone number, but he was not successful. Ten years after my father's demise, my uncle was invited into a home in Bangalore—this is my mother's brother, my dad's good friend and confidant. He was attracted to a large painting in their living room.

"Do you know something? I am not an artist but my brother-in-law who is an artist paints in a style similar to the picture you have hanging in your living room. You don't mind if I take a closer look at it, do you?"

"Please be my guest and go right ahead," said the man.

My uncle was shocked as he recognized the signature on the painting. He immediately turned around and confronted the man. "Where did you get this painting?" He knew that his brother-in-law had made no sales, and he wanted to know if this man knew the artist and had received this as a gift from him.

"I paid a lot for this painting. I bought it several years ago in Madras," said the man.

My uncle told him that we were trying to retrieve all of the paintings by this artist so that they could be returned to his family estate. "I don't mind buying it back from you," he implored. But my uncle was unsuccessful, and we knew who'd sold this painting.

Another time Appa had an exhibition where my uncle's friend was interested in purchasing his painting of a woman with a calf. Amma asked, "Are you sure you want to part with this painting?"

"Well, I have never made any money selling paintings," Appa replied. "Maybe the tide has turned and this exhibition is going to start a new trend in my life. I may turn out to be one of the few artists who will die wealthy from selling his paintings."

"I somehow don't trust this man to be an art lover," said Amma. "After all, I have lived with you long enough to appreciate art and know who loves art."

"Don't worry. I think he wants to present his wife with this painting for her birthday," Appa said.

"Well, I think this painting reminds me of your mother's love for calves and cows. You should hold on to it," objected my mom.

"If it was left to you and my mom, I would paint away and keep them arranged in the attic where no one would set eyes on them," said Appa.

Anyway, this man was very interested and walked off with the painting after paying my father a small sum of money. Ten days later he called my father and said, "My wife is now very unhappy, and she feels that this woman in this painting is coming between her and me. She told me that I was spending too much time staring at this painting and she wants to get rid of it."

My highly disappointed father took his painting back from the man to save the man's marriage. My mother was happy that the painting was returned. One woman's loss is another's gain. It hangs in my living room.

I remember Appa most for the portraits he did. When we were children, we used to frequent the house of Appa's boss, William. He was from London and had the brightest pair of blue-green eyes. His wife told Appa that she would love to give her husband a painting for a gift. So she commissioned Appa to paint her husband. Now Appa had to copy from a photograph of William. This man was in his sixties, and the picture was of him when he was in his thirties with a beard. Appa was not a portrait artist, and his confidence level was dwindling when he heard his family commenting on the painting as it was being created. First of all, Appa did not believe in optics or copying. His was a free-hand drawing of a thirty-year-old man, but it was not William's face. Appa was highly disappointed with our input, so he erased the canvas and restarted the drawing from scratch. He consoled himself and us: "Once I start to paint, William will be easily seen on the canvas." I bet he struggled through the painting, as he refused to show it to us after our criticism of his initial attempt. It was finally done and he spent time framing it himself. A white cloth covered the painting, and I did not even take a peep, as it would disrespect Appa's feelings. He had told us that the first person who should see it should be William's wife, and we could see his point. We were invited for dinner at William's place. Dad took us all for the inauguration of his painting. We could not wait to see his wife present the portrait to her husband.

William's family and friends were gathered to celebrate his sixtieth birthday, and all were eager to see the painting. My dad was the maestro at this party, and we were all gloating. Finally the time came for the white cloth to be removed from the portrait.

"Oh my God! I just can't believe what a wonderful job you've done," William's wife enthusiastically patted Appa on his back. "He's so handsome, and he did look like this when he was thirty years of age. I even remember the bow tie that you have neatly painted around his neck."

The blue-green eyes were beautifully depicted; the beard had some blond, brown, and gray streaks, which was quite realistic. This painting was of a handsome young man in his thirties who could knock any young woman down silly with lust. I could see why Appa did not let us see the painting as it was being created. It was some other William. This was not William my dad's boss whom we'd known very well for the last few years.

"Is this what age does to you?" whispered Amma to Appa. "He was so handsome. I wish that you could have shown us the photograph. I just can't believe that it's him that you've painted."

Appa agreed happily with William's wife. "Moham, beauty is in the eyes of the beholder. William's wife swears by my painting. She says this is the likeness of her man, whom she met thirty years ago. Who am I to question her? Her imagination is still green and her love has gone up a notch thanks to my painting."

The birthday party was well celebrated, and Appa's artwork was even more celebrated. When we returned home, Appa confessed to my mom, "I don't think I painted William. I painted William's wife's imaginary boyfriend, the one that will make her fall in love all over again with her William." Appa was now an artistic accidental cupid.

He tried to paint my mother a few times and gave up. "I can never paint this most beautiful woman. She cannot be recreated on canvas," he said. He won many brownie points with Amma. The only painting of me by Appa is where my mother is teaching a disinterested child, which happened to be me. He never tried painting any of his children.

CHAPTER 3
Dad Meets Mom

> Soul mates are people who bring out the
> best in you. They are not always perfect but
> are always perfect for you.
> —Author unknown

The college where Appa did his agriculture degree is located in Guntur district. Andhra Pradesh is like many parts of India, a state where agriculture is the chief source of economy. This "rice bowl state" is an ideal location to learn all about agriculture. Appa was young and eager, and he spent a lot of time in the beautiful paddy fields. These lush green acres were flooded with water. The beautiful women spent a large part of the day planting young paddy plants, their saris up to their knees lest they get wet. This is a common sight when one travels through the Guntur district.

Appa and his friends spent a large part of their time playing cricket on their days off. The other days, he and his gang of buddies got interested in a plant other than rice: tobacco. This was the first place that Appa not only studied the plant, but also enjoyed it occasionally on a social level.

"Your son is getting into bad habits, I hear from his friend's father," reported Thatha to Patti after having taken a stroll down the street, where he met Shivarama's parents. "I think we have to have a talk with Ambi," he continued.

"Shivarama's father is a good-for-nothing man. He has no right to talk about your son to you. What about *his* son? He thinks his son has no bad habits at all?"

"Who knows, and I don't care. All I'm interested in is making sure that we keep a close watch on Ambi. The next time you speak to him, let him know that his allowance will be cut and he'll not be able to spend it on the wrong things."

"What big bad habits could he be having, that you have to stop his life line?" Patti protectively argued for her son. "Poor Ambi only has Mantharas and Naradhas around him. He should just stop getting involved with this *kadankaaran* [a man living on borrowed time] Shivarama." (Naradha is the sage in the well-known Mahabharata mythology. He is considered to be a troublemaker. Similarly, Manthara is the woman in the *Ramayana* who brought about the banishing of Rama to the forest for fourteen years.)

"I think it's time to get him married. That'll teach him some responsibility."

Appa's parents' intuition into his behavior was it was curable by marriage. The wedded state would make Appa differentiate between what is right and wrong, and Ambi from then on would be accountable and rational. He would successfully complete his obligations and duties toward all concerned. This may be one of the reason there were so many marriages in India and the population soared. Once it had been deduced by Thatha that marriage made a man responsible, feelers were sent out to procure a bride to make Ambi responsible. If Ambi failed in his responsible duties, the wife would by default act responsibly, and if she failed to carry this dutiful act for the couple, then children would arrive, and so on and so on.

Patti and Thatha did not waste any time. They started looking for a bride. Well, I was not born to oppose this proposition. For the first half of my dad's life, his parents decided on the color scheme and subjects that were to be painted on his life's canvas. For the second half of his life, the brushes and paints were doled out by his wife and children. So, I was partly responsible for some of the strokes on his canvas.

Shivarama was not Appa's friend, but his prattle landed Appa on Thatha's radar. Something good would definitely come out of this snitching. The net for a bride was cast beyond Tamil Nadu state.

Amma had no idea that she had been detected by a master radar apparatus. Amma was a beautiful, innocent girl growing up in a boarding school in Benares. Unbeknownst to her, her parents had been contacted by this common friend Dorai Mama (Uncle Dorai). He spoke highly of Thatha and Patti. He could not stop praising their son Ambi.

Amma was sixteen years old, enjoying her life in Benares attending tenth grade. Little did she know that her dad had communicated with Thatha through Dorai Mama, and her school days were soon to be something of the past. My mother's dad, Guruswamy Thatha, was eager to get her settled. I do not know if he evaluated the horoscopes or the eligible bachelors when it came to finding grooms for his two daughters. Amma's mother, Veda Patti, was uncomfortable with her husband's decision making in the marriage field. Moreover, the astrologer had warned Guruswamy Thatha that he did not believe that Ambi's and Moham's horoscopes matched.

"I think that you are wrong," Guruswamy Thatha told the astrologer. "What does one need to make two horoscopes to match?"

After giving 50 rupees, some beetle leaf and beetle nuts, and flowers for the astrologer's wife, the astrologer happily announced that it was a great match. Venus, Mars, Mercury, and the Saturn were all in correct places in the horoscope, and the stars were a great match, and if your daughter did not get married to this man, she might remain a spinster. At least bribes worked to my dad's favor at a celestial level, and a match was made. Thank god for small mistakes and bribes—my sisters and I had our parents decided for us by an unreliable astrologer.

Amma and her parents soon made a trip to Madras and temporarily rented a place there. This home belonged to a famous Carnatic singer, V. V. Shadhagopan. He constantly practiced and even tried to get my mother to learn some music from him. He tried to impress on her how she should have a couple of short songs ready to sing for the guests. The day had been set for Appa to meet Amma. Amma was a shy sixteen-year-old girl dressed beautifully for this eventful day in a pink sari. She never wore makeup, and that day was no different. Her hair was parted on the side. That was the fashion in 1949. She wore a simple gold chain, bangles, and earrings. She never believed in putting kohl in her eyes. She did complete her dressing with a traditional red dot on her forehead.

Appa, Patti, and Thatha arrived for the official *Penn parkkum padalam* ceremony: seeing the prospective bride. Guruswamy Thatha and Veda Patti had outdone their hospitality. The place was decorated and there was every variety of goodies that one could dream of. The two main items that were musts on those ceremonial days were *sojji,* a sweet made of cream of wheat, and *bajiyas,* batter-coated fried vegetables. These were served sizzling hot.

Appa was curious and walked in looking for Moham through his rimless glass. He had thick straight hair combed and held slick with Brylcreem. His intelligent eyes were roving through the room eagerly looking for the girl, whose photograph had made his heart skip a beat. She was not waiting in the living room. After the guests had settled, the appetizers were served. It was time to invite Moham into the living room. She shyly walked into the room with some coffee in her hand. She did not dare look up to see her future husband. She was nervous. This is not something that she had been trained to do. How on earth did you train a sixteen-year-old girl to act coy for a *Penn parkkum padalam*? But she aced it, and despite her lack of experience, she had stolen the heart of three people who were in the room.

Thatha, of course, liked my mother instantaneously. My dad did not even have to nod to show his pleasure and approval after seeing my mother. But how could you not fall in love with this charming person? She must have been drop-dead gorgeous too as a teenager. I am not boasting about her looks just because she is my mother, but anyone who meets my mother thinks that I am not her child. We were overshadowed by her beauty and charisma. I would get annoyed when anybody pointed out the differences between my mother's looks and mine. I did not want to look like my father, but I did.

Anyway, Thatha was not just a businessman. The film industry had trained him and he had a good eye for a pretty girl. Moham, as a daughter-in-law for the family, would be the right subject in the colorful canvas. The very next day, he came over to finalize the liaison between the two families. He did not want this beautiful bird flying away to another nest.

"Mr. Guruswamy, my wife and I had a long discussion about Moham. She is the perfect mold for our family. My son Ambi will make her happy. As you know, we are well endowed, and we do not need any dowry. All we want is your daughter, and the wedding can take place at our home. There is just one thing; my son has not completed his studies. She will live with us after the wedding, and as soon as he gets a job they will be able to move into a place of their own. I give you my word that as long as I am alive, your daughter will be taken care of." Thatha, a gentleman, kept his words till he took his last breath. He adored my mother, and in his eyes she could never do wrong. When he was upset at my dad's nonchalant behavior, he would confess to my mother. "I told your father about my son. You are too good for him. But your father did not heed.

He wanted you to get married to Ambi. Did your dad ever confess to having this conversation with me?"

Guruswamy Thatha did no such thing. When I was a mature woman of Swamy's household, I was privy to some of the family secrets. I found out that he marched to his own drums. He had no heart-to-heart talks with anyone. He also did not believe in giving any options. For that matter there were no discussions with even the older brothers and older sister before he decided that Moham would marry Ambi.

So, without conferring, the wedding date was fixed. He did what he thought was right. If he had been my dad's father, I just don't know how the DNA chromosome twist would have unraveled to create all of the unborn Swamy clan.

Delighted by the sudden change of direction he had created for his daughter's life, Guruswamy Thatha returned home with flowers and sweets from the local store for his wife and daughter and announced that he had agreed with Padmanabhan, Ambi's father, to conduct the marriage before the end of the year. He received no go-ahead from his wife or daughter, but the wedding date was set.

I don't believe Moham was interested in getting married, and who would be at age sixteen? Her peers all over the world were going through the postwar transformation and were meeting and mating the Western way. Here she was in Madras introduced to a family of seven brothers and sisters. Soon she was to betroth to the oldest in this family. She was not all that naive and was not unaware of what was happening around the world so far as marriage and love went. Her parents, particularly her father, believed that marriage was not just a union of two people but an occurrence in one's life where *families* united. As far as love went, it would eventually grow like branches and buds on a tree. She, on the other hand, had been seeing Hindi movies where the lovesick couples were running around trees and dancing and singing while professing their love to each other. She also had seen doom and gloom in these movies where parents had arranged marriages. Especially when the parents do not heed their children's likes and dislikes marriages, can fail.

Moham was disheartened by Ambi's appearance. She was like any teenager of her time absorbing every detail about what happens in romantic movies, and Ambi did not fit this romantic mold. Have you ever seen Dilip Kumar wooing Meena Kumari while he models a *veshti (loin cloth)*? The only consolation was that these two tragic king and queen movie stars from yesteryear never did make it to the marriage *mandap (altar)*. There were villains and parents who placed unforeseen obstacles and tore the lovesick hero and heroine apart in almost every movie they acted in. My mom, for one, did not want to be a part of such a tragic union. After all, they will be planning a family should this marriage materialize.

"I don't want to marry," my mother protested. "Why do you fall for their wealth? Just because they are prosperous, it does not mean I should get married into this family. I don't want to be sacrificed on the marriage altar just because you want to hand over your responsibilities as a father and let some other man take over your job of taking care of me." My mother knew that she had a weak chance of putting this off. Her father was ailing from complications of type 2 diabetes, and he feared that if he did not do his duty as a father then, his unmarried daughter would have difficulty.

But what family listens to a teenager? The wedding arrangements were going full swing.

We always jokingly told Appa that he got lucky. If he had asked for a dowry, he might not have gotten Mother and might have been a bachelor for life. He was never fazed by all of us chiding him about his nuptials or for that matter the least amount of input that the two of them had to join in holy matrimony.

"Appa, there is no way we are going to allow you to have any hand in arranging our weddings," I said. He was relieved, for he did not want to worry about us. But I think he left it to his sister, who actively spent her life recruiting men for women who had sworn spinsterhood or men who planned to venture into the life of a *sanyaasi* (hermit).

Ambi had his own doubts about getting married to Moham too. He wanted his life mate to be in his frequency and enjoy music, sports, the arts, and reading. "Appa, I don't think Moham knows how to sing Carnatic music. I would like to marry a woman who has some knowledge in music and arts," Ambi related to his father rather shyly. What transpired was a call from Thatha to Guruswamy Thatha. What do you know? Moham and her father drove up to the Marina beach in Madras, and Ambi and Thatha met them there. Marina beach is a beautiful, long, sandy beach along the eastern coast of India, which is also known as the Coromandal coast, which means "black sandy beach." Ambi, as usual, did not believe in the Western style of wearing a pair of trousers, and so he was dressed to represent the Madrasi culture in a *veshti,* or *dhoti,* as it is referred to by the Indians who live in the north. It is a simple white piece of cotton soft muslin wrapped around the waist.

Looking back, I could see my mother's reaction. She was a teenager from the north, where they are exposed to men in pants. Moreover, she had been to Hindi or Bollywood movies and knew exactly how her man should look. The main heartthrobs from Hindi movies when she was a young teenager were Dilip Kumar, Dev Anand, and Raj Kapoor. She wanted her future husband to be a combination of Dev Anand's height and charisma, Dilip

Kumar's smile and flamboyancy, and Raj Kapoor's sense of humor. These stars did not model a *veshti* in a romantic spot like the Marina beach. Who had ever seen a heroine being chased behind an Indian mango tree by a hero in *veshti*? Even though she was a Madrasi brought up in northern India, this public display of casual dressing in a *veshti* turned her off. Well, teenagers today are more vocal about their likes and dislikes, but my mother, a teenager in the late forties, lost her tongue when she set eyes on the hero who was to be her life partner.

"Moham, did you learn to sing Carnatic music?" inquired Thatha, as he wanted to make sure that his son Ambi had no doubts.

"Yes," Moham said, to their relief.

The fact was that when she was six years old, a music teacher came to her home to teach Carnatic music to my mother and her sister. They hated this man and hid outside in the garden as soon as they saw him. He was a cruel task master, and when he did catch them, he did not spare their thighs. He would toss in sand from the ground on their thighs and give them a pinch for being playful when they should be eagerly practicing their songs prior to his arrival. My mother hated this teacher, but there was no one in that village to replace him. She did learn music, but at six years old her interests lay elsewhere.

Relentless Brush Strokes

"Ask her to sing a tune for us," Ambi requested his father to ask Moham. Does that not sound funny? He did not even dare address her directly. That was the forties in India, when dating was unheard of. Imagine how modern my grandparents were to have taken their twenty-six year old son to meet a sixteen year old at the beach. This was groundbreaking for those days; the second fateful time that Moham and Ambi spent together with chaperones—when marriages in India were held without any approval from the bride and the groom. Moham had friends who saw the man they were about to marry at the *mandapam* (wedding altar) for the first time. She considered herself fortunate to have seen him twice before the fateful day.

Amma did not remember any of the songs taught by the abusive Carnatic teacher. She was modern and current in her music appreciation and decided to choose a song from the latest Hindi movie playing at the local cinema house. After all, the man she was about to be betrothed to was from a family that made movies. They must be connoisseurs of all kinds of movies, pop culture, and film music.

So she sang a pop music verse. Thatha and Appa did not comment. Thatha was a smart man. He was not about to veto this beautiful girl just because she did not sing the tune that his son wanted to hear. Ambi would have all his life to teach her to sing his favorite songs.

"Appa, Moham does not know how to sing. Are you sure she is the right one for me?"

"My son, she is the most beautiful girl, and how does it matter if she can sing or not?" Thatha replied.

"I don't think she even knows Tamil that well," fussed my dad. "I cannot stand this Hindi language. She seems well versed in a language I do not care for." (As a student, a large part of his day was wasted carrying a placard that said GET RID OF HINDI.)

"What do you want from a wife, my son?" Thatha countered. "Do you want her to sing Carnatic music or take care of you, your home, and your children? Have you heard your mother singing around the house all day, or is she busy attending to her children and home? She will fit into our family."

The two families did not waste any time, and before the end of the forties, my mom and dad tied the marriage knot.

CHAPTER 4
Wedding Day

> Marriage ceremony: an incredible metaphysical sham of watching God and the law being dragged into the affairs of your family.
> —O. C. Ogilvie

According to my parents, the wedding celebration lasted for five days. I have no idea what they did for five whole days. But I have a pretty good idea of some key elements, and I will give a digest of what went on during the fateful days of October 23 and 24.

October 23 was the day when Ambi, the groom, was welcomed by the bride's family, in a ritual the South Indians refer to as *Maapillai azhaippu,* welcoming the groom.

Guruswamy Thatha presented to my father a suit, watch, and diamond ring. These were a must before the *Maapillai azhaippu,* even though Thatha did not insist on any dowries. This was just a token present from Moham's family, and they insisted that Ambi accept it. Believe it or not, if the customary formalities and presents were not doled out by the bride's family, the bridegroom (not Thatha's family) might not arrive at the *mandapam* the next day. This was not about to happen, as Ambi had reconciled to the fact that Moham was not a singer, and she was not about to be a professor of Tamil. She had not asked any questions of him either, which was great for him. But in her heart of hearts, the nagging question was still, "Does he own a pair of pants?" Well, what did she know at the age of sixteen? Moreover, Ambi's astute and smart father knew that Moham was the best person for Ambi.

To avoid sticky situations, almost all arranged marriages have a wedding coordinator, or a family *athai*—a father's sister or some close friend of the two families. This coordinator can break or make the situation. If she disliked the bride or the groom's family, she would simply weave stories and try to make the day miserable. To put it in plain words, with the wrong person organizing the wedding, one does not need any enemies to blotch the already strenuous day.

Ambi was in his element. He decided to choose his own suit for the *Maapillai azhaippu,* a cream-colored one, the color that my grandmother professed looked best on him. His mother must have played a big role in the choice, or that was the latest for the fifties. Not Moham's choice of color. I still remember the suit. Appa did not have the heart to discard it. His weight never changed, and he would wear it whenever there was a special occasion. In fact, I did not even ask what the occasion was, as my father would sometimes wear it and we would tease him about his fashion sense.

The *Maapillai azhaippu* is traditionally held the evening before the wedding. Ambi sat in a decorated convertible sports car with his four-year-old sister on one side and his six-year-old brother on the other. He had a rose garland around his neck and looked handsome. He was ready and on his way to the temple to seek the blessings of God before he ventured into marriage.

Ambi's friends Raman and Sambandham gave a knowing wink. He knew exactly what they were alluding to, as he got into his father's decorated convertible.

"Finally, you get to sit in the passenger seat and be a groom, Ambi," said Raman.

"Hey, don't say it too loud," said Ambi. "My sister and brother are all ears, and before you know it, the story will travel from your lips to my father." He was popular amongst his classmates. Who would not be, with a father who had six cars and an imported British convertible sports car, which, unbeknownst to his father, Ambi would generously loan to his friends. Many of his friends had their own *Maapillai azhaippu*s in this car, and to save money, Appa would dress up as the official chauffer.

On one such auspicious day, for Thatha's family friend, Ambi had allowed for the car to be decorated. Ambi's friend warned him that his parents had been invited to the wedding. "Don't worry," consoled Ambi, "for I have told my parents to just attend the wedding, and not come to the *Maapillai azhaippu*. My mom knows about it, and she has promised to keep my dad busy in the backyard, as and when the wedding procession passes our home tonight."

By the way, it is considered bad luck to see the bride the day before the wedding, and my parents did not see each other. Mom's brothers, Paddu and Chotu, fourteen and twelve years old, respectively, were the messengers for the day. Her sister Jayam was eighteen and pregnant and could not be by her side for most of the time. Paddu and Chotu were not too sensitive as to what a woman liked to hear on her wedding day. All they knew was that their sister, confidante, playmate, and best friend was about to get married to a man she barely knew, and if they could only ask her to say, "I am not going to go through with this!" then all would be back to normal. She did not have to go through this ordeal, and she would be back to playing with them.

Relentless Brush Strokes

October 24 dawned, and the wedding hall was a bustle of activity. My mother looked beautiful in a rusty brown sari with a red border. She just followed orders and never questioned as to why she was getting married when she was just a teenager. She did all that was needed to change from a teenager to a married woman. I am still surprised that my mother did not question, for she has taught me otherwise. I guess this was her first day at the practical school of how to say no and not take nonsense from others. She ventured out of protective parenthood to stand on her own two feet.

But Paddu and Chotu were not making this separation easy. "Moham, are you sure that you want to get married?' asked Paddu. "Dad is quite an understanding man. If you start to cry and beg of him, he will be able to put a stop to this wedding madness."

"Paddu, don't be crazy," said Moham. "He has spent a lot of money. There is no way we are going to back out. Decent people don't do such things. Honestly, Paddu, you have got to grow up. Jayam got married too and she is going to have a baby. You did not protest then. You will get married too someday."

"Then, why are you not smiling like the movie stars who are so happy in the pictures on their wedding day?" asked Chotu.

"You both should just get lost and take a breather," scolded Moham. "I am not interested in talking to you, and Mom and Dad will get upset if they hear you."

"Mom, Moham is crying," said Paddu jokingly.

"I am not crying, you silly monkey," Moham wept.

"My God, you don't know how to cry small drops of tears, do you?" asked Paddu. "Here, we can collect a bucket. Now you are going to get us in trouble!"

"Speak for yourself! I did not make her cry," accused Chotu.

"Paddu and Chotu, stop teasing your sister," their mother said. "She has to be ready to go for the wedding *mandapam*. Leave her alone."

"You still have an hour to back out, Moham," reminded Paddu, as he tried to gesture and gyrate with his body as to how Moham had to walk into the *mandapam* in front of hundreds of people.

"Amma, Paddu is bothering me," cried Moham. "He is teasing me and making fun of me!"

"Moham, you are sixteen years old, and a big girl about to be married," scolded her mother. "Please act mature and stop being playful. Soon you will be a wife and you cannot be chiding around your brothers."

Ambi had arrived. He was making his way into the *mandapam*, the wedding banquet hallway. The musicians had started to play the *naadhaswaram*, an Indian horn, and the drums were beating in rhythm. All were ready to start with the *Kashi yaathrai,* a make-believe pageant in which the groom pretends to leave for Benares to become a monk. The bride's father stops him from going and begs him to marry his daughter, as a monk's life is no comparison to wedded bliss. Guess what? Ambi is no monk. I was not there, but he would not be able to live without Moham in Benares. They speak Hindi, the language that he cannot understand. Who will be the translator? He would need Moham at Benares.

"Look, Moham," Paddu shouted gleefully, "he is coming in his *veshti*! I just don't understand why we South Indians have not learned to dress up like the North Indians in *sherwani* and *kurtas* for a wedding. It would be more elegant."

"Paddu, I do not need your running commentary about how my future husband looks," said Moham. "Just keep quite or get lost."

"Don't be so testy," Paddu replied. "I am only trying to make you less tense. If you want me to go away, I will, and you won't have me next to you. I will leave you by yourself, while you sit in front of the fire amongst all those priests."

"If you stop making silly comments, you can stay, okay," said Moham.

"I love you, Sis," said Paddu, with tears in his eyes. By the way, my uncle Paddu does not need any coaxing to cry, especially if it has anything to do with his sister, whom he loves unconditionally.

The fateful time had arrived. Several large metaphoric canvases have been prepared and laid for creating a new family unit that is predestined. After all, this is my parents' lives that are being portrayed, and one never knows how many offspring they may have. The powerful colors were chosen by the two families. The symbolic brush was in Ambi's hand; it was a bright and beautiful October day, and the cobalt blue, violet, and titanium white were blended together and applied by a palette knife to add texture and drama to the dancing clouds. The white, fluffy clouds were slowly added to the forefront in a mixture of titanium white and cobalt blue. My dad never liked zinc white. He said titanium white was far superior to blend with other colors. Not a gray in the sky. The special canvas blended the two partners, culturally diverse in their upbringing, having grown up in two different parts of India and decades apart in their age. The indistinct nebulous orange clouds made the sun shy when it saw the most beautiful women in the *mandapam*. The *mandapam* is the representation of a temple altar where a God and Goddess are to be married. The center of the metaphoric painting was Moham in the *mandapam,* as she sat on her dad's lap during the *Kanyadhanam* ceremony. The literal meaning of *kanyadhanam* is "maiden donation." But philosophically speaking, the bride's family is asking the groom to protect their prize in a symbolic offering. For my wedding I asked my father not to donate me, as I did not believe that it was easy to give me away. I prefer the ritual being reworded as "tying of the knot."

The wedding had cooks brought in from some of the best towns in southern India. No less than a thousand people attended the wedding. Guruswamy Thatha did not ignore any details. He was an ailing man with complications from diabetes. This made it quite uncomfortable for him to let his daughter sit on his lap. She was well aware of this, and she gingerly perched herself on his knees while she arched forward for Ambi to tie the *thali* (yellow thread) around her neck. I have never seen my mother without this *thali* for forty-three years of her life.

The celebration was grand, and at the end of the day Moham innocently asked her father if she could return to her own home and to her own bed. At sixteen I cannot imagine the confusion she must have gone through. Her sister, who had been betrothed at thirteen, had returned to school after her wedding, only to be teased by her classmates. My mother thought that she would be attending school too.

"No, my sweetheart, you are now married, and you will be going to your in-laws' home," said her father. "You can come and visit us when they allow you to. I will come and visit you next week and see if everything is okay with you." He had tears in his eyes as he gave her a hug and a kiss before he let go of her hands. Guruswamy Thatha adored his children, and unlike many fathers from the forties who would not display their affection outwardly, he was always ready to hug and kiss his children in public.

Paddu and Chotu were not making this separation easy. They told her, "If you are not happy, let us know, we will bring you back!"

Ambi had his own dilemma. He was still a student, and he had come to attend Deepavali at home. He was now married and had nowhere to take his bride. He would have loved to take her with him, but that was not meant to be. He was returning to school, and his wife was to spend the time at her in-laws'.

"A stroke of luck" or "a brush with fate," call it what you will. Ambi had a combo of the two phrases served on a silver platter, or on a palette, which is what he would have preferred. His brush was loaded to mix the right colors to be dabbed onto his fateful life canvas. His lucky brushstroke was ready to render a masterpiece. As some seers may say, you have no control over your destiny, but you can certainly change the strokes and the picture frames. This my father did as and how he pleased. The young bride from the *mandapam* was ready to be transferred onto another fateful canvas.

She was his beautiful, demure wife ready to face the immediate challenges of the future, in a place where she knew no one and with a bridegroom who would be leaving for university.

CHAPTER 5
And Then There Were Three

> The most terrible poverty is loneliness and
> the feeling of being unloved.
> —Mother Teresa

University was far away from Madras, and it was not easy for Ambi to return frequently to see his new bride. He tried to visit her. He wrote letters—and that must have been tricky. Moham did not read Tamil, and Ambi did not know Hindi. The letters must have been in English. She could understand and read English, but she could not express herself in English fluently.

> My dear Moham,
> I have not spent too much time with you, but I feel as if I know you well. You have changed my life for the better. The interview at Brook Bond Tea Company went off well. I cannot wait to settle down with you in Kadamane estates. I have received my job

offer and I am sure that you will like this place. I will be back in May and prepare to leave for Kadamane estates. I miss you.
Yours loving
R. Swamy

Appa always signed his letters formally, and I don't believe that Amma and Appa had any nicknames for each other. Amma addressed Appa as *ennah*, an endearing way of addressing a husband amongst South Indian women. He often called her *yaar*, an endearment meaning "buddy," "pal." Her reply to his letter was:

My dear Ennah,
I am waiting. Take care of your health. I am happy and we will go together to Kadamane.
My *namaskar*, greeting to you.
Love,
Moham

I did have the opportunity to read one of the letters that Amma wrote to Appa. She had trouble expressing herself in English, and her letters were literal translations of Hindi or Tamil:

My dear Ennah,

Everybody is fine here. I am sure you are fine there. I have good news for you. One of Savithri Mamis husbands friend has job in Poona. You know man. Mani is mans name. Ennah, before you return Mani with wife and children leaving for Poona. They are sad before going to Poona, that they will not see you.

Loving,

Moham

Lalla, please correct this for me. Otherwise, your *appa* will tease me about my English," Amma said.

"Amma, I will laugh with my sisters before Appa does."

"Please don't tease me," Amma said.

We three sisters corrected and rewrote the letter and finally asked Amma to copy what we had written for her, before she posted it.

"Your *amma*'s English is improving," Appa happily commented on his wife's penmanship in English when he returned from his office tour. "You are all attending a Catholic school, and it looks like she is getting better."

As soon as Appa returned from university, he and Amma took off to Kadamane estates. He had a brilliant career at Brook Bond Tea Company in Tea Estates, located in the hills near Coimbatore. They had a beautiful home, and his gardening talent made it a most beautiful place. Cars would stop to look at the tasteful garden he had created. I was a baby and I do not remember any of these. But I have heard about this place so much that my imagination has been tweaked. Moreover, Appa loved to talk about the flower steps that he had created. These were colorful flowering plants separated by evergreen shrubs. Even though I was too young to have remembered any of these things, like most children who have heard stories of their childhood related by their parents I visualized these situations over and over again and have almost deluded myself to have experienced them.

I also believe in a powerful statement made by my secretary at our clinic: "I only type what I hear." Every report that went out of our clinic had to be corrected, and those were the days when typing was done on a Brother typewriter. She would use White-out and hand-correct the mistakes. When we confronted her about messing up every report, she replied, "Doctor, I only type what I hear." I thank you, Rene, for your quote. I am also writing what I heard.

"Moham, we are going for a party to my boss's place. They have asked us to bring our daughter along."

"Are you sure you want us to take her? It could be late and we do not know if this will cut into her sleep time."

"Don't worry, she will be okay," replied Appa. As they were returning home from the party, the car came to a standstill in the middle of the jungle, as Appa had forgotten to get gas.

"Moham, you stay in the car and I'll walk over to my boss's place and get some help," Appa said.

"No! I'm not going to sit here by myself. What if there are tigers or leopards in this dense jungle?"

"Don't be silly. There are only elephants that I see, and I can hear some wolves and the distant roar of a lion," Appa said.

"And you want me to sit here by myself, while you walk into the roaring lion's arms looking for petrol?"

They waited for two hours huddled in the car, and it seemed like a day. They let the horn blow continuously and watched the elephants slowly walk in herds beside their car. Finally a man with a hurricane lamp in his hand came upon them and saw their problem. He helped Appa fill the car with some petrol, and they finally returned home.

Amma hated the Kadamane estates. The tea estate was located very close to a large forest, and at night the spooky sounds from the jungles kept her awake. To top it all, they had a nut living upstairs. His name was Mr. Pain, and he was clearly a pain in Amma's neck. He was an avid collector of exotic snakes, and he let these reptiles slither around on the floor of his home, which happened to be our family's roof. Amma was petrified and was sure that one of these days she and her beautiful family would be a delightful meal for the python, or their death would come from the toxic venom of a cobra. She had even seen a thirsty tiger loiter in our backyard looking for water. That was the last straw. She contacted Thatha and let him know that she was terribly scared of this place when Appa was at work, and she did not want to be alone with her baby.

Thatha came to her rescue and told his son Balram that this was no way to bring up a child when the wife was suspended in a state of terror. My *chitthappa* (my father's younger brother) drove out to Kadamane and picked up Amma and me. She was back in Madras at her in-laws'.

This was a groundbreaking moment in Appa and Amma's relationship. It was the only time Amma got away with it. She actually took her own brushes and gave a few strokes to Appa's symbolic life's picture as she envisioned a less adventurous and more stable lifestyle for their family. The separation did not last long, as Appa could not bear to live without Amma. He was back with her in Madras.

"Moham, I cannot live in Kadamane without you and Lalla. I have no reason to live there by myself," Appa said. He left the job and was back in Madras at his parents' place. He did not like doing this, but he had no options. His wife and child were already there.

"In that case, find another job, as you do not like living in Madras," Amma advised him.

If there was a reason why he held on to his jobs, I for one would say it was largely due to Amma. She would in no uncertain terms let him know that if he left his job for any reason, then we could pack up and leave for Madras. He might as well live under the telescope that his father had held focused over him. That was the last thing he wanted. His heart was set on art and painting, but he continued to go to work. He was a reluctant white-collar worker. His interest always lay elsewhere. If anyone had walked up to him and said, "Swamy, why don't you give up your day job and paint some landscapes for me?" he would have given it up in a heartbeat, no questions asked.

When I say that Appa was not able to live without my mother, I truly mean it. He could not sustain himself. When she went to visit her brothers just to get a break, he would use any pretext to have her back. In those days he did not believe in calling. He sent her a telegram. The telegram would read: "Moham. Seriously ill. Return."

A full sentence in the telegram could cost a pretty penny. These four words, however, conveyed the true meaning of a man who was critically ill or was eagerly waiting for some critical altercation with his wife when she did return speedily. The "ill" part of the telegram was a figment of his imagination that mobilized even my skeptical *amma,* who was well versed in his modus operandi. What do you know? My mother did catch the next train back to be with her dear husband.

"Amma, I bet you he's okay," I comforted her when I was old enough to understand the serious situation and was privy to this many times.

"He always does this when I'm away for a few days."

"But, Amma, don't you believe that Appa may be really sick?" I asked.

"If I didn't know him as well as I do, I would say that Appa is seriously ill and admitted to the hospital. But Appa is infuriating me so much that one day I'm going to ask him to go to Madras and let his family deal with his juvenile behavior. Nobody will tolerate his immature behavior like I do."

"Amma, he's nowhere in the house," I announced as soon as I entered it.

Amma walked up to Dr. Hazra's clinic to ask if her husband had visited him, and the doctor knew nothing about any illness in our family. He had not been admitted to any hospital. Now she was angry with Dad and his feigned illness. She waited for him to return and wanted to blast him with her most venomous words. It all fizzled and evaporated when she saw him walk in through the front door holding on to his chest.

"Why did you make me return?" she demanded.

"Look at me. I'm unable to walk and I had palpitations and chest pain. I thought I had a heart attack," he said.

"You look fine. How did your heart attack get cured?"

"I sent the telegram and then I went to the pharmacy and got myself some medicine," Appa said. "The gas in my chest and belly was pushing at my heart, it seems. But, I'm glad you came back," he said sheepishly. I was already next to Appa, and my sisters and I were glaring at Amma for not being sympathetic. When it came our turn to deal with his "gastric reflux mimicking heart attacks," we understood why Amma reacted in this fashion. She was well aware of his hyperacidity being fueled by his tobacco. She wanted him to give up this habit.

"What is that package in your hand?"

"Oh, that's left over from the food I had at the South India Club," he said. "It's greasy and not good for my acidity. But I couldn't help it, as I was hungry and there was nothing to eat at home."

"I'm sure you're late coming home because you had a game of bridge with your friends too?" My mother was quite mad and rightfully so.

"Forget it, *yaar*. I missed you and the children, and it's too boring without you all in the house. Please don't leave me alone anymore," he implored.

The household was back to normal, my mother had forgiven Appa, and we children were happy to see that he was healthy and okay. I could not fathom why Amma let Appa get away with this malingering.

Appa sometimes gave in to quick tempers, which we saw projected mostly on Amma. I was told that when Amma was in labor with me, a Dr. Shanmugham did not show up on time and I was caught by a midwife. To top it all off, the doctor did not even prescribe the correct medications for Appa's bundle of joy, which did nothing but cry to keep the household revolving around her demands. Anyway, this led to some friction.

"Doctor, you may not know it, but I was a medical student for three years," announced Appa with anger. "The reason I gave up medicine was to avoid being a doctor like you! You didn't show up for the delivery, and now you have no clue as to why my daughter is crying all the time."

"Swamy, there is nothing wrong with your baby," the doctor assured her. "You are carrying her constantly and she is getting used to your body warmth. She is attention seeking and wants to be hugged and snuggled by you all the time. If you give in to her, you are going to suffer." The doctor had found out that Appa spent all night sometimes lying down with his daughter on his chest. He could not bear to leave her in the *thooli,* a cloth cradle, lest she cry. "Well, suffer Swamy, for your folly," the doctor said under his breath. "Your little baby has already wrapped you around her little finger and you have no hope in hell. Let her cry. It's good for her lungs."

Appa was mortified by this reaction to his precious little doll, the sunshine of his life. She was going to change his life for the better. How dare the doctor speak in this way? "Moham, I'm not complaining about being up all night with my baby," Appa told Amma. "What if she had something seriously wrong? I want Dr. Shanmugham to refer her to another doctor, as I don't think he's an expert at children, let alone delivering babies."

"Don't be so blunt," Amma corrected him. "He must be a good doctor. Your daughter is getting spoiled by you."

"Well, I won't be calling on you for any more services in this family," Appa declared to the poor doctor, dismissing him.

Prema was born, and Amma had no major issues with the doctor or Appa. Along came the third pregnancy. Amma was excited, as she related to me several times when I became a mature lady. She said that her pregnancy felt different. These were the days when there was no ultrasound or amniocentesis to confirm the sex of the baby. The whole family was looking up to her to provide a son for the Swamy clan. She was 99.9% certain that this time it was going to be a baby boy. She did not have much morning sickness, and this time she felt less heavy and did not look or feel radiant as women bearing female children do.

By now, Appa and Amma had moved to a small town in southern India, Vadapadhimangalam, where Appa was a manager at a sugarcane factory. I remember going there once with him. I was only four years old, but I remember big hills of sugar. Appa searched high and low for a doctor to deliver his third child.

"Ennah, I think I'm in labor," Amma announced. "Shantha's mother just had a baby and she might know of a doctor. You have to find a doctor who can come over to our place."

"I'm on my way to our neighbors' place," replied Appa as he left to bring home a doctor for Amma's delivery. He was back with the doctor in an hour.

"Moham, we are very lucky. Dr. Shanmugham has been transferred to work in our town," Appa announced. Appa had to eat humble pie and bring in the same doctor who had delivered me, the one who did not think very highly of my attention-seeking abilities. He was back to deliver Swathi. I do remember the day my sister was born. She was the most beautiful baby that I had ever seen.

"Prema is crying, Amma," I said. "She wants to sleep with you." Prema and I were hoping to edge our way into Amma's bedroom, as we wanted to be with the newborn. We were curious and wanted to hold this small baby.

"No! You both have to sleep with Appa," Amma's mother told us. She wanted her daughter to take some rest, and pointing to the placenta and umbilical cord, she said, "You both should leave your mother alone, as there is a snake in the room." So much for going near my mother after my sister was born.

"Moham, I'm very happy that you're safe after delivering our third daughter," Appa told Amma. "But how are we going to pass on this message to my father?"

"I'm scared too. Two daughters in an Indian family is a welcome addition, but this third one . . . I was so sure that it was going to be a son," said my mother disappointedly.

"I'm too scared to send a telegram," admitted Appa. "What do I say in the telegram: 'Moham gave birth to another daughter. Mother and child safe'? I have a better idea. I won't send a telegram. Instead, I'll write a postcard to my mother." And a postcard was penned by Appa to Thatha and Patti:

> My dear Amma and Appa,
> We are happy to announce that Swathi was born under the star Swathi, and she is extremely beautiful. Her sisters are very happy, as they can play with her. I do not have to worry about any new clothes, as I have a lot of baby girls' clothes. Your

daughter-in-law is extremely happy. My chanting of *Lalitha Sahasranamam* has paid off with three beautiful girls in our family. We could not ask for more.

We seek your blessing on the auspicious occasion of the naming-of-the-child ceremony that is to take place soon.

Your respectful son,

Ambi

Upon hearing the good news, Patti made *payasam,* a dessert made with milk, and drew a big, beautiful *kolam*—a decorative design made of rice powder—in front of the family home. She announced cheerfully to all the neighbors that Ambi had had a third daughter.

"What is the occasion for the *kolam* and the *payasam*?" Thatha asked when he arrived home from work.

"I just got a postcard that Moham gave birth to a beautiful daughter, and all are fine!" Patti announced excitedly.

"It is not a son, and this is not the first child," Thatha rebuffed her.

"What does it matter, a boy or a girl? She is another Lakshmi-God of wealth in this family. So it is time to celebrate."

Thatha replied to his son's letter immediately:

Relentless Brush Strokes

My dear Moham and Ambi,

I am glad to know that you have all celebrated the arrival of your third daughter. Ambi needs to become more responsible, as it is not easy to bring three daughters into this world. Education and marriages need to be conducted. Moham, I leave it in your responsible hands to make sure that your husband is gainfully employed and supports the family. I hope that Ambi understands that it is a serious and responsible role that he has to assume as the father of three children.

Affectionately,

Appa

Thatha was never far from the truth. He was asking too much from my easygoing father. He can be serious and he can play roles, but to play a role as a serious and dependable father was asking too much of him. Moreover, Thatha was asking Amma to be the parent to her own husband and make him responsible. I believe that this was what Thatha had meant before Appa got married to Amma when they were contemplating their son's marriage—marriage to make him responsible. This was no easy job for Amma. She already had her children, and now Thatha was bestowing his son in Amma's hands. At times Amma did play an active role of a parent to Appa.

Amma took ill with typhoid and was unable to attend to her three children and the family chores. Her brothers were not sure if she would make it through this sickness in a small town with no proper health care. So she was taken away to her family home in Calcutta. Amma left with Swathi and Prema. I stayed at Thatha's place.

Yet another new figurative life canvas has been laid in front of Appa. This time the challenges were different. His wife was far from him and his one daughter was living at his father's place. He would not be able to live without his wife and children. There was no way he was going to duel with his father. He left his job and off he went in pursuit of my mother for the second time. This time he left for Calcutta and I was happy to see that I was accompanying Appa to be with Amma and my sisters.

CHAPTER 6
Thatha's Telegram

> God grant me the serenity to accept the
> things I cannot change, the courage to
> change the things I can, and the wisdom to
> know the difference.
> —Reinhold Niebuhr

I do not know how many of you have lived during the telegram period. Telegrams were the means of communication in India during my childhood. They were the "e-mails" of yesteryear (or e-mails are the "telegrams" of today). There is no drama to writing an e-mail, or for that matter opening one. But, a telegram puts a spin to its message, as it concisely conveys its meaning on a white streamer printed with words, stuck by glue onto a pink form. It was never a complete grammatical sentence, as the number of words dictated how much one was going to pay for the telegram. An express telegram spelled a more expensive and urgent notification by the sender.

Telegrams were always treated as bearers of bad news in my family. We did not believe in the telephone, and these telegrams had a way of waking you up in the middle of the night. The knock on the door and the stranger shouting "Telegram!" when you were in deep sleep punctuated your life with vivid images of all that could be wrong or could go wrong if you opened that piece of paper that this stranger was about to hand to you. These strangers were handpicked by the telegraph office. They boasted the persona of men who delivered court subpoenas. Our home was not immune to these telegrams, and God alone knows how many I saw delivered at our doorstep.

"Sri Ram Jayam, Bhaghavan, Ram's victory, oh God—please let there be no bad news," Amma fretted, following Appa to the door. By the way, during the daytime Amma would open the door boldly to any stranger, but when the sun set she would hide behind Appa, the poor slight man, who would open the door to all strange knocks. Now, if you have seen my delicate, slight *appa,* you might think twice about letting him do this. But, I guess it was okay in our safe neighborhood, to admit a stranger bearing a telegram for our family. As soon as Appa received the pink slip, he hastily tore it open the wrong way, and now he was busy trying to reassemble the pieces of this jigsaw puzzle.

"Ennah, why can't you be in less of a hurry and open it carefully with a paper knife?" scolded Amma as she was impatiently waited for the news. Trailing behind my mother was her brood of three, all eager to know what disturbed the harmony of this magical night's slumber.

"Today it is good news," Appa replied with a sigh of relief and a smile. "Balu is getting married." Balu was his younger brother. "Moham, the telegram man is the bearer of good news. Please give him a bag of rice." Thatha made sure that his children got a supply of rice sent from the family farm, and Appa was generous in sharing.

We danced around excitedly, as it meant that we would be able to go to Madras and have a good time with uncles, aunts, and cousins. I had already started to imagine what I was going to wear for my uncle's wedding. Appa and Amma started to discuss booking the train tickets.

"Tomorrow, I'll talk to Swamy and ask him to buy the tickets," Appa said. Swamy was our neighbor who worked for the railways, and we did not have to go to the station to pick up the tickets.

The next day, Amma was busy preparing for the trip. This wedding did not give the relatives enough time to think. We had to literally toss our belongings into our trunk and make our way for Thatha's place. Appa was the oldest, and this was Balu Chitthappa, Appa's younger brother, so you can imagine the excitement.

Then another stranger came to our door and announced, "Telegram." This time it was a bright sunny morning and Amma was not afraid to open the door. Moreover, Appa was at work, and no one else could receive the telegram.

"Sri Rama Jayam, Bhaghavan—let there be just good news," murmured Amma as she opened it. The pink slip was another one from Thatha. It read, "Presence not necessary."

My mother stood shocked. Here we were preparing to leave for Madras. What kind of an invitation was this to the eldest son and his family? Were we not expected to be there? Did he not want a family reunion? Was it not true that weddings were more for the pleasure of the friends and families than for the bride and groom? Was it not the meeting place where families and friends exchanged exciting news and gossip about each other and took trips down memory lane? What went amiss in twenty-four hours to change Thatha's mood from a man about to receive his son with open arms to one displaying rejection?

Thatha loved his children and sent them sacks of rice or money if and when they needed it. He expressed his love for his children and grandchildren by actions more than words. The wedding was an occasion that spelled crowds, expense, and chaos. Thatha must have asked Patti, "Does Ambi have to transport his family all the way to Madras? It does not stop there. An entourage of family members will have to make a long trip to Madhurai, as the wedding is not taking place in Madras. This is too much to coordinate for just a two-day affair. One has to be sensible and practical. It is not necessary to take time off, especially when Ambi has just joined this new job. His boss may not be too sympathetic. It is not like anyone has died and his presence is required."

"Moham, Appa does not want for us to gather for a good occasion," my father later commented. "Now, why would you think it's only important to attend funerals and not weddings? I am known to not listen to my father. I respect his opinion, but I'm not about to let my brother down," Appa said authoritatively. "So, Moham let us prepare for the trip. We are going. I don't care what he says." The dynamics between Appa and his father always led us to believe that the distance between them lent enchantment to the view, and that may have been why Appa was in Calcutta while his siblings lived in Madras. Appa did not have to be told what to do, especially now that he lived far away and fended for his own family. The choice had been made, and we would follow our Appa to Madras.

I loved my father when it came to decision making. Any other man might have said that this was the last time he would have anything to do with his father. Enough was enough. He announces a wedding by one telegram and then asks you not to attend the wedding in the next. He might as well have not sent the first telegram. Not Appa. He did not take such snubs lying down. He had desensitized himself to his father's slights. This piece of pink paper somehow was not received as an insult by Appa.

But Amma was panicking. She tried to tell Appa that we should not go where we were not invited.

"I would not go if it were a friend or a distant cousin. But this is my younger brother who is getting married. I will not miss it for anything," Appa declared.

The wedding was on; our trip was on; and who cared what Thatha said in the telegram? Appa had already prepared his hot fantasy red period painting of happiness and weddings on his large bright canvas with reds, yellows, and oranges. The wedding depiction by Appa is what I see as he makes me imagine the day with his palette knife and brushstrokes.

"It must be a mistake," Appa remarked consolingly. "It should have read: '*Presents* not necessary.' The attendant at the telegraph office must not know English."

Well, this was the response from Appa: A cat's meow for a lion's roar. So, the five of us left for Madras.

CHAPTER 7
Madras Express with Mom

There are many memorable trips that one may take. I for one remember the trip that we took for Chitthappa's wedding. Now that I consider myself to be a seasoned traveler, I cherish some of my earlier travels by train. The anticipation and excitement that energized our family home still flows through my veins.

Appa had made his decision, and we were getting ready to leave for Chitthappa's wedding. The days are cool in Calcutta, and January is a pleasant season in Madras. We three children were no big help when it came to planning for the long trip. The "whole enchilada" was left in the capable hands of my competent mother. She single-handedly made this a successful journey. To think back, I wonder how she did it without any help.

Appa was another story. If the planning of the trip was left in his hands, we might have gone somewhere; and I can tell you with no uncertainty that it would not have been to Madras. There was a better chance of not going at all, which would have brought tears and disappointment to Amma and us. So, I assume that the trip preparation was left in the capable hands of my super-Amma.

These trips were not easy feats. The clothing's for Amma, Appa, and three children were neatly packed into heavy trunks. When I say trunks—these were made of stainless steel or some complex durable metal that was so heavy and cumbersome that no traveler needed to worry about anybody snatching it. Even then, Amma slept lightly in the train with one eye open, I am sure, to stop any such mishaps.

(If I remember correctly, such a mishap occurred to my parents when I was a year old—and guess who was being carried around the streets of Mysore with her bottom in full view for all at a street fair, where my parents were eagerly awaiting for the Maharajah of Mysore to appear? I am glad I do not remember the day or the embarrassment.)

You can imagine my mother's anxiety in preparing for these trips year after year. We almost always went to Madras in December. Our trunks were packed, along with a "hold-all," a canvas bag in which our bed linens and blankets were packed for the trip. For our return trip, this hold-all would hold dirty linens too. Then Amma had to make some goodies to pack for the trip as well. Even now her DNA molecules carry these codes. She packs her meals for her trips on flights. What do you know? Mothers are always right. With airlines providing no or unpalatable food, she and her well-trained DNA are ready with the right lunches and dinners for her long trips to Madras from Toronto. There are some Indian ladies who hover around her on such trips to Madras, when she gladly shares these goodies and has her own plane parties.

My mother was ready with her three children to take off for our long-awaited exciting trip to Madras. The only person missing was my dad.

"Amma, Appa is late. Are we going to miss the train?"

"He's probably on his way from work. We have no way of contacting him."

In the sixties, there were no cell phones to remind absent-minded Appa. Retrospectively, a cell phone might have regulated my father's absent-minded digressions. Our fear was that he might have forgotten that we were leaving for Madras. But not this time—he arrived from work at the eleventh hour; we all packed into an ambassador taxi, and off we went to Howrah Station. Those cabbies never came alone. They always had a passenger helper who sat in the front with the driver, and as it was a bench seat and my dad was lean, he sat in the front and we sat in the back.

"I want to sit by the window!" I yelled after Prema, who always got her way and yet again scampered off successfully to get the window seat. Running was not my forte, and she beat me to it. "I don't want to sit in the middle. I want to sit by the window, Amma," I pouted and complained as I took my place beside Prema, and my mother got in and placed Swathi on her lap.

"Now, you don't start giving us trouble. There's enough tension with your Appa being late," Amma told me off and glared at me. Of course, I could not see through the window where my mother sat with Swathi covering the window, and Prema had ingenious ways of not letting me peek. I did not want to start any brawls with Prema as my mother glared at me, widening her eyes to their full dimensions.

My mother simply opened her eyes wide and her glare was enough to send chills of fear through us and we'd behave and not cause any trouble. Her controlling capability is still unique and never fails. Corporal punishment was never used in our family. Our behavior was modified by mere penetrating stares from my mother! My children tell me that I have learned this technique from my mother and effectively use it to let them know my displeasure at their behavior.

The fun started at the Howrah Bridge. There was no way we would be able to reach the station in time. The traffic was at standstill; but if we missed the train, there was another one called the Janta express. *Janta* means "people," and express meant that it would go at a snail's pace. The Madras express took 36 hours, and the Janta express would do the same trip in over 48 hours, stopping at all small stations on the way. We had no confirmed sleeper arrangements, for the Janta express, which meant that we could have been sitting all the way for two days should we fail to catch the Madras express.

My mother was worried and was loudly saying her prayers and invoking God to assist in this Howrah Bridge traffic jam.

"Amma, look, we are on the Howrah Bridge," I excitedly pointed to the bridge over the Hooghly River.

"Guruswamy Thatha built it," Prema said. She was trying to become my pal, as I had given her the cold shoulder over taking the window seat.

Calcutta and the city of Howrah were separated by the river Hooghly. Howrah was a busy port and had a railway station. In the late nineteenth century, when Calcutta was still the capital during the British rule, a lot of attention was paid to this city. The river Hooghly had a floating pontoon bridge erected by Sir Bradley Ford in 1837. This bridge allowed for transport of small vehicles and buffalo carts. World War II demanded marching of troops between Burma and India, and this small pontoon bridge could not have handled the flow of traffic. In 1937 the construction of Howrah Bridge began, and several construction companies were awarded the contract.

Guruswamy Thatha was the chief engineer who managed the construction of the first cantilever bridge in India when he was working for Brathwaite, Burn and Jessop Company. This great piece of architecture was completed in 1943 and is 705 meters long and 97 feet wide. The interesting piece of information about this great bridge is that the steel framework expands to a meter in the height of summer. I have heard about this so many times, but as a child my brain decoded this piece of information as if my grandfather had erected it single-handedly.

"Amma, did Thatha do it all by himself?"

"Don't be silly," my mother would correct me on many occasions. "Thatha had thousands of engineers and technicians working with him."

The traffic jam over the Howrah Bridge was making it difficult for the cabbie to maneuver, and it looked like we might not make it to our train. We had a coolie porter carry our monstrously heavy trunks all the way across the bridge to the train. Several cars and taxis had emptied their passengers and luggage, and the coolies, having heard of the traffic jam, decided to cross over to the bridge to assist the outgoing passengers. These poor coolies or porters did not have trolleys, and they had to carry the load on their heads. The bartering to get this coolie to do it for a cheaper rate deserves a separate novel. My mother, tactfully with her engaging smile and

Relentless Brush Strokes

caring ways, got a good coolie to help us amidst this sea of people and coolies with luggage on their heads now streaming along toward the railway station. If the traffic jam had originally been caused by the volume of cars, now it was due to chaotic crowds running helter-skelter, making any automobile movement impossible.

Finally, we reached the station, we children hurrying behind our mother. And my mother was hurrying behind the coolie lest we lose our luggage. We reached the train inspector's side, where there was a crowd of travelers asking him where their seats were. In her authoritative voice, my mother announced, "I'm traveling on my own with my three children and need to know my seating arrangement!" That got the attention of the train inspector. One thing about Calcuttans, they respect women, especially if they are by themselves with children. It must have been from my mother's lips to God's ears, for she had come with Appa and announced that she was alone with her three children. My father was suddenly missing. We could not see him anywhere. For the inspector, who assigned seats to the train passengers, it appeared that this young lady was traveling alone with her three children.

"Amma, where is Appa?" I started crying, as my father was not to be seen and the train was going to leave in five minutes. We were already seated. My mother was irritated with Appa's irresponsible and unbecoming behavior, especially when he had three young girls and a wife to attend to. He was nowhere to be seen.

"The Madras express is about to depart platform two in five minutes," the announcement came loud and clear. The train slowly started to creep.

"Amma, the train is leaving the station. Appa is not here," I was bawling my eyes out, with my sisters accompanying me in stereo. I was six years old and they were four and two. That Dad may be lost forever had not dawned on my two sisters. "Amma, you have to pull the red rod to stop the train for Appa's sake," I urged, driving my mother insane with questions about how we were going to get hold of Dad.

"Shut up, Lalla," she finally told me, and added, "He will be coming by the Janta express, as he has missed this train."

After an exhaustive three hours of whimpering over Appa not being there and the excitement of the travel planning that I finally fell asleep in my mother's lap. The train rolled to a slow stop at the Kharaghpur station. This was the city where the first Indian Institute of Technology (IIT) was built. It was a place that could be proud of having produced many of the great engineers of India. Kharaghpur was the train station where my lost Appa returned to our train compartment.

"Amma, look! Appa is here!" I excitedly ran toward him as he stepped into our compartment when the train came to a halt at Kharaghpur. I was ecstatic to see my father join us. My mother refused to speak to him or hear any of his excuses. I still remember—he had bumped into a long-lost friend at the Howrah train station, he said. We found out the next day that he and his friend had joined a large group of travelers to play cards and enjoy the long, tedious haul to Madras with.

CHAPTER 8
Chitthappa's Wedding

> Marriage is an alliance entered into by a man who can't sleep with the window shut, and a woman who can't sleep with the window open.
> —George Bernard Shaw

Finally, after 36 hours in a coal-powered steam engine train, with small coal particles entering our eyes and irritating them continuously, we reached Madras Central Station at about 4 p.m. My grandfather had sent his car, in which our young Balu Chitthappa came to pick us up at the railway station. Our happiness knew no bounds when we saw our uncle. We all forgot the small escapade that we'd had with our father and his disappearing act at the railway station. We embarked on renewing our ties with our uncle, whom we were very close to. We were excited about his upcoming wedding, for which we had made this long trip.

Chitthappa drove us to our grandfather's palatial home. We were quickly dispatched to clean up, as our clothes were almost black from the soot deposited on them by the train, and our face had a gray hue.

Thatha's home had an interesting boiler that made hot water for bathing. It was a large double-barreled shiny copper vessel. The inner barrel was filled with dried kernel and coconut husks which were kindled to produce fire. The outer barrel was filled with water. There was a spout at the lower end of the outer barrel from which we drained the boiling water into a bucket and mixed it with cold water before use. People who took their baths were responsible for filling the emptied water boiler. There were times when everyone played truant and the responsibility fell on Thatha to take care of the boiler. If there were no water in it, it might get a big hole from the high heat and would need major repair. We kids were exempt from this duty, as we were too small to deal with heat.

Patti, an excellent cook, had made a very special meal. It was Appa for whom we thought she held a special spot in her heart. After all, he was the firstborn, after five years of childlessness in the marriage. She had been written off as a barren woman by some of her kin and friends. Now, who in their right mind could identify any barren woman, especially in India, which boasts a population of one billion? God knows how many children are born every second in India. I can safely aver for my family that we may not have multiplied like rabbits, but we were a second close. My grandparents had seven.

What can I say? Our neighbor's kids beat us fair and square in the numbers game of how many brothers and sisters they had. I can say with almost smug confidence that between our two families, we have littered all five continents with our feel-good, feel-strong chromosomal bonds. Our cosmopolitan family from interracial marriages now shows exotic beauties from all permutations and combinations that one can perceive. In the fertility department, our family confirms that we have no problems.

Now, Appa and Thatha did not discuss the telegrams that were sent. Appa did *namaskaram* to Thatha and Patti, and all seemed well. Thatha was visibly happy to see his son and family. There must have been a mistake by the clerk in the telegraph office—instead of "presents," he must have written "presence." The British taught English to the Indians; but post-independence, Indians clearly showed signs of deterioration of their English-language skills. India was changing the medium of instruction from English to Hindi in North India, and all states were making schoolchildren learn the state language.

"Thatha, we lost Appa in the station," we excitedly conveyed to my grandfather about Appa and his meandering away at the station.

"Girls, could you come here," called Amma as she gave us her glare. She did not want any of the information percolating to Thatha, an authoritative man who exemplified dignity and discipline. "Don't tell Thatha about Appa," Amma whispered into our ears. This could erode the pleasantries that were being exchanged by father and son.

Now, who in their imagination would have thought that my grandpa was the father to my absent-minded, free-spirited *Appa*? This was nature's way of creating an aberrant twist to the chromosome, to flaw Thatha's ideal family picture. My father, the oldest son and heir, whom my grandfather had hoped would lead by example; was a carefree, easygoing, fun-loving, yet somber man. Nobody followed him, for he did not believe in leading. He had trouble keeping his hooves from trotting off in different directions from the rest of his body. He was a true genius and could have belonged to the Mensa Society. His interests lay in painting, the arts, music, books, philosophy, religion, metaphysics, history, and the Upanishads and Vedas. These were just a few topics I remember discussing with Appa over the years. He was a great teacher, a lover of art and music. He did not have the time to be like his father and act dignified, well composed, and leaderlike.

Finances, focus, fortune, and family were Amma's department. She would conceal any of Appa's actions that might have produced raising the eyebrow and from being frowned upon. The last person who should hear of any of his misdemeanors was his father. We were too innocent and small to know the depth of reaction or repercussion that would ensue from exposing Dad. Thatha controlled the purse strings, and he deserved to do so, as he was a self-made millionaire. Appa, on the other hand, with his inherent weakness to be deviant, might have been labeled the "black sheep," with grave consequences. For Amma, this had to be avoided at all costs.

"Thatha and Patti, I want a pretty silk *paavadai* [petticoat] in green," I announced as I danced into Thatha's formal entertaining room. Thatha was seated on a big chair where he spent a lot of time. This was a large room that had a small study with a table and a telephone to one side. It led into the main large room, where people were entertained. If they were Thatha's professional friends, they would go straight to his formal room. This had large sofas and a desk. He had his big portrait hanging on the far wall next to his parents' photographs. The windows looked over the garden, the front foyer, and the verandah.

"Of course, you and your sisters will have pretty *paavadais* for the wedding," said Thatha and Patti.

The next day, the silk merchant arrived at our grandpa's home. My grandpa had no qualms about spending money on his family. We were all lavishly treated to silk dresses for the upcoming wedding. He loved his grandchildren; I was his special pet and thoroughly spoiled by one and all. I got a beautiful green *paavadai*.

Appa and Amma planned to make a religious offering during this trip. It was not easy to keep making those long trips from Calcutta. A wedding, a religious promise, and visiting cousins, uncles, and friends was a lot to be accomplished in a month, and the wedding was smack in the middle of our holiday. Anyway, they decided to speak up and mention this religious offering to Thatha.

Appa, a God-fearing man, went meekly to his father and decided to break the ice. Appa might have been the father of three, but in front of *his* father, who displayed a commanding presence and oozed self-confidence, even a lion would only purr or timidly let out a meow.

"Well, Appa, I have a personal commitment to go to Tiru— Tiru— Tirupati," my dad stuttered. He went on to explain how this was not something that had been planned by him.

"Who asked you to take such absurd religious oaths?" demanded Thatha. Despite the aura of disbelief at Appa's religious pursuits that Thatha exhibited, he always wanted to know who the culprit was for any situation brought on his family, not instigated by them. His children also knew how to palm off their responsibilities to somebody else, so that they did not have to singe alone in Thatha's wrath.

Appa immediately stumbled in with the explanation. This was Appa's way of passing the buck to his brother-in-law, my mother's brother. "When I was going to take Swathi to the local barber to give her a haircut, Ramu stopped me and said that she deserves to be taken to Tirupati for her hair-shaving ceremony. I could not stop him in midsentence. Now that he has uttered the big ceremonial hair offering, how else could I stop him?" But the big "but" is why for a third daughter? Hair offering is typically done in many Indian households. It does not have to be at Tirupati, it could be at Pazhani Malai or any other temple. Nothing out of the ordinary for a Brahmin family, I suppose. The first haircut is always done at a temple.

"He must be crazy to suggest something as outrageous as this," retorted Thatha. Thatha made no bones about religion, and he held my father totally responsible for bringing on this issue of hair offering at Tirupati.

"But one cannot break a promise to Tirupati," Appa pressed on hopefully.

The whole family was in an uproar. Some sided with Appa and others sided with Thatha. The main religious person in this brood was my father. He believed that all Godly promises should be carried out or else the karma would be borne by all generations to come. Our understanding about this issue is that if you do not keep your promise and offer your hair to Lord Venkateshwara at Tirupati, then he had his own way of taking what you have promised him with an added penalty.

Now you have to look at this from Thatha's viewpoint. As he went on to say: "What is so special about doing this for a third daughter? It was not like after two sons you got this gift of a daughter that you should offer her hair to the God in Tirupati. You have had two daughters and then you were hoping for a son. But that did not happen. Moreover, who in their right mind would offer their daughter's hair just before a wedding?"

Appa would. He could not have sons but that didn't it matter. Hair is hair. My parents were proud of their three daughters, and they planned to educate them and bring them up like sons! Moreover, he was a God-fearing man. "Appa, I do not like to go back on my sacred pledges, and it is not easy to come to Madras just for this ritual that can only be done at Tirupati," Appa continued to stand by his words.

But Thatha was willing to play Russian roulette and poker with God and let God's wrath unfold. His feeling about all this was that it was religious claptrap. What if you didn't offer the hair as promised? So what? Will God take your hair away from you if you do not offer it voluntarily? It is only hair, you silly people. It will grow anyway.

Hair may not have been an issue on Appa's side of the family. All of Thatha's family had a crown of hair, and alopecia was never a dinner table topic. On the other hand, my maternal uncle Ramu, who had conferred with my parents to offer my sister's hair at Tirupati, had a shiny scalp, and to him this breach of promise to God could lead to serious implications for his sister's family's tresses.

"You cannot chastise Ambi over his religious beliefs," my grandmother came to my father's rescue, and she was almost sent with my sister for a shaving ceremony to Tirupati. My grandmother was upset at my grandpa's lack of sensitivity toward religious rituals. All said and done, my grandpa might not have been religious, but spiritual he was. He did not believe in wasting time in front of a temple to wait in line to see the idols, and the last thing he would do is to line up at Tirupati or Swamy Malai for a religion-based hair-removal ritual. But he enjoyed collecting flowers for his little altar every day. He expected men to show their substance by action and not by tinkering in a temple. He also believed that the duty of a Brahmin was to chant his *Gayatri Jappam,* a chant done by men to attain salvation in life. So, he was not all bad or an atheist.

"Look at this pretty girl. She will now have no hair before my wedding," my *chitthappa* moaned, upset that Swathi would now have to attend his wedding with no hair when all the other little girls and her cousins would be wearing flowers in their hair. It did not bother Swathi. I do remember my sister wearing the flower around her shaven head at the wedding.

Grandmother was too preoccupied with all the other happenings. She was glad that my parents finally won their way to Tirupati. My sister and I stayed back with our grandparents and were taken to the village, where Thatha owned a large piece of land. The reason for this trip was to make sure that our pregnant cow Raji, who might deliver any day, needed to be cared for during our absence. So, we left Raji in the care of the farmer, Chelvan. During the wedding, Patti was preoccupied with thoughts about Raji. "I hope that we will be back to make sure that her delivery is easy. I am worried about poor Raji."

The wedding was a gala celebration, where we had a lot of fun. As children, we had no responsibility. Our aunts had us all dressed up and we were flitting around like colorful butterflies in the wedding banquet hall. My uncle had met his wife-to-be only once and had decided that she was the one. She was a beautiful woman, and her wedding sari and jewelry were simply grand. My mother was beaming from ear to ear, proudly showing her three children to friends and family who had gathered.

We returned the next day after an exciting two days at my uncle's wedding. The fun had just begun. Raji was brought back to Patti's care. She with Gopal and Amma were busy in the backyard in the cow stall. Raji was in labor. She was crying out big moos and we could hear Patti singing to her and coaxing her to take it easy.

"Raji, now you can do it. You are a big girl. This is not your first. Now I am here for you," coaxed Patti. The West has heard of "horse whisperers," but I know my grandmother was a cow whisperer. She could make any cow do anything she wanted. I could see that Raji was slowly becoming quiet, as I sat on a big block of hay waiting earnestly for the calf to arrive.

The ground had been covered by sacks made of jute. This was taking place in the corridor that led to the garage. I could see that this was a religious event. There were flower garlands, fruits, bananas, incense, camphor, and lamps being lit, and my mother and Patti were going around Raji saying prayers. They had the candle in their hands. Before they went around twice, Raji gave one big moo, and without much ado there was the most beautiful calf that was born. He was trying to stand up as soon as he came into the world. He could barely see. The afterbirth and amniotic fluid had made the spot so slippery that I was afraid the newborn calf might fall. But I was warned not to go near the calf, as Raji could get aggressive and butt me fiercely.

My grandfather saw that all was calm and wanted to know what was born. My grandmother proudly announced that it was a male calf and would be useful at the farm when he grew up to be a bull. She may have been disappointed that it was not a cow, which could have given milk, but she did not show it.

"Now, why is it that we have an excess of bulls in our cow stall?" remarked Thatha as he looked at my father teasingly. "We have no lack of females in our cradles." My dad did not take the bait. In India, where the cow is considered a sacred animal, there is rejoicing at its birth—whereas, when a female child is born, there is a different sentiment. The families consider this addition to be a burden, as they will not be able to help on the farm to the same extent as sons can; and daughters' marriages are expensive, as dowries have to be doled out. We were too overwhelmed watching the birth of a calf, a miracle. My father's opinion in this issue was how does it matter if it is a boy or a girl? A woman's labor of love is never lost. Way to go, Appa!

CHAPTER 9
King of Cricket

> We don't stop playing because we are old;
> we grow old because we stop playing.
> —George Bernard Shaw

If Appa and Amma were disappointed in not having a son, this was not apparent to us three. We accompanied Appa on his cricket trips and had a great time. We looked forward to the weekends, when we did not have to go to school. My friends told me about how they were allowed to sleep in and their parents would have a gourmet breakfast and so on and so on. It was a little different at the Swamy's residence. Appa would be up at 5 a.m. before the cock crowed and would have the morning pot of coffee flowing like a brown stream down the kitchen counter. Amma had not woken up, as she did not have to get the kids ready for school. Surely she deserves to wake up late two days in a week. It was not really a day off for Amma. She got up every day at 5 a.m., and today she would rise at 6 a.m. But my dad could not bear to see my mother sleep in. His puttering around the kitchen was not noise free. It resonated throughout the household. In his hurry to cover up the mess he had made in the kitchen, he clumsily wiped the counter and in the process knocked the coffee and filter onto the floor, and my mother hurried down to see what the din was all about.

"Why can't you wait till I get up and make your coffee?"

"I did not want to disturb you, as you looked too tired," confessed Appa as he saw the mess he had created.

My mother is territorial when it comes to her kitchen. I am wrong. My mother is territorial when she sees *any* kitchen. It does not have to be her kitchen. It could be in any home and anybody's kitchen. The owner of the home will not even know that my mother, with her sweet smile, is capable of translocating any housewife from her kitchen. Nobody knows our mother's motives as well as we three sisters do. She cannot stand the dietary regulations that we throw on her. Her way of doing away with diet is to take over the cooking. She also feels that our bodies and bowels are regulated by only her meals.

"You have created such a mess!" Amma confronted Appa.

He wore a sheepish grin and told her, "Forget about it, *yaar*." Using his "buddy" approach was his way of asking my mother to take it easy when she had to make the coffee again and clean up the mess made by my dear

Appa. This mishap did not dampen his enthusiasm about the weekend, which was action filled. This did not include his wife. It may have included the children. He quickly got ready after his morning prayers.

Appa was a changed man after his prayers. He shed all religious garb and was ready to hit the cricket ball. He wore his white trousers and shirt and was ready to leave for the Eden garden, a large park in the heart of Calcutta where he would be meeting his friends to play a day's match. He was hurrying my mother to get his breakfast and coffee ready. "Moham, I don't want to be late, as I will miss out on the warm-ups and the practice with the coach."

"I'm making a small breakfast."

By this time, the noise and the aroma of morning *dosas* being fried in the kitchen had woken all of us up. *Dosas* are Indian crepes, crispy and tasty, served with coconut chutney and sambhar. Appa was whistling away and was very happy, hitting imaginary balls into the air.

"Appa, we want to come with you," we begged Appa. "Please, we'll behave ourselves."

"I have no problem taking you with me."

"But who will take care of the children in the park?" my mother put her foot down. "I can't send them with you where there's no adult supervision." God knew what could happen to three young girls in a park. This problem was resolved very quickly; Appa's friend and our neighbor came to pick him up for the game. His sons and daughters were going with him, and he saw no problem with us accompanying his children. So, my mother had ready-made baby sitters and was happy to have some free time while we went to watch Appa play cricket.

Cricket is an interesting game with eleven players on each side. Appa was a bowler, and after every display of his prowess, he would look toward his children for their approval and admiration. In our eyes, he was the best bowler, but the other side was just too strong and he was unable to get the batsmen out. Soon, he was displaced and made to stand far away from us, and I was a little miffed with the cricket captain, for I thought that this was not fair to stop my dad from bowling. Finally, we returned worn out and hungry from the long day. Appa's team did not win, but they were good about it. They made up with the other team over beer and *samosas* while we kids were treated to ice cream.

Appa was a good sportsman. He always felt that he was an important member of the cricket team, and not having won this time did not dampen his enthusiasm. We largely owe our interest in cricket to him. The five-day cricket matches that were played in India were followed by the cricket fans largely on the radio. There was no television, and we could not afford to go to all the matches. I remember the one time that Appa got tickets, the game was rained out and our money was refunded. It was sad to see Appa's downfallen face when he came home wet and disappointed.

When Appa could no longer bowl for his team, he was not ignored by the younger crowd that had taken over. They would come over and ask Appa to be an umpire. We three teenagers at home would eagerly eye the youngsters who would come to our house and had our own nicknames for them. Well, Appa liked to dress for the job.

"What do you think of this for an umpire?" he asked, wearing my doctor's lab-coat, as I was a medical student. He would model my lab coat for the Saturday and Sunday cricket matches and ask us for our approval before he left for them. We did not hang around his cricket games, as it was not cool to follow your father when you were a teenager, and we preferred our own friends by then. He used to be a little disappointed, but he understood. I am sure he wished that he had a son.

The final match between Australia and India was on at the Eden Gardens. This large serene park on the banks of the river Hooghly in the heart of the city was another creation of the British period. The land belonged to Maharajah of Cooch Bihar. During the British era, Governor-general Lord Auckland held this large lush wooded area and tended to the garden. He relinquished it to the city for public use in the late nineteenth century. The first Calcutta Cricket Club was established in 1792 in Calcutta by the British. This is considered to be one of the oldest teams outside of the British Isles, having participated in many great games that have made history. Eden Gardens is not just about the stadium. It has an artificial lake by which stands a beautiful pagoda, erected in 1880. It is unusual architecture for this country, brought to India by Lord Dalhousie when the Burmese army was defeated.

If you know anything about India, we do not take cricket lightly. We take it a step further than just winning a cup. It is not like the Stanley Cup of hockey, where the excitement dies in a week. If you win an important cricket match in India, the fans will convert all those who do not follow cricket into fans. It is a national holiday and traffic comes to a standstill due to the chaos that hits the streets. You only have three options: (1) You go to the game to see your team win and not reach home due to traffic; (2) you go to school and spend the afternoon huddled in the gym listening to the game on the radio and as soon as India wins hit the road and stop all those who want to do something else by bringing the entire city to a crippling halt; (3) you do what Appa did. He bought no ticket to the game, but he was not about to go to work and miss out on the cricket match commentary when it was do or die for India.

The World Series is a five-day match and the two teams play two innings where each team gets its turn to bat and bowl. On the final day of the series, the second inning was beginning, with India batting. The Indian team had not done well in the first inning, but there was hope that they may recover.

So here was Appa at home mustering courage to tell Amma that he didn't feel like going in to work today. "Moham, I'm not feeling well. I feel like I'm coming down with something. I didn't sleep well, and I may have some stomach upset and diarrhea. My chest pain is also acting up, and I want to take it easy."

For my mother, who is an expert at diagnosing diseases caused by real bacteria and differentiating them from the "not wanting to go to school" malady, was immediately aware that Appa wanted to take a 'French leave'. She didn't approve of such deviance from the norm but had to give in. She knew that her day was going to be busy. He must have other tricks up his sleeve. Sharp at 8 a.m., even though he was not going to work, he took a shower, said his prayers, and was sitting in front of his radio, tuning it to the right channel so that he would not miss Vijay Merchant's commentary on the teams before the beginning of the game.

Now, the radio was a different story at our place. We had two or three of them, and all had their covers removed and were always standing upside down in a "repair me" position. None of our radios ever functioned, thanks to my father. He took great pride in his degree in radio engineering and experimented on all these gizmos constantly. To top it all off, friends and neighbors trusted him with their radios. At any given time, there were seven to ten radios all eagerly waiting for his attention. He may have successfully fixed them, but on the day of the big cricket match, our three dying or dead radios were not about to squeak anything into my father's eager ears, least of all the cricket commentary.

Not to worry, as we had one too many people in our neighborhood who loved my father. He put on a sad, puppy-dog look and walked out. Our neighbor Sen saw his fallen face and came out immediately to ask, "Uncle, what's the matter? You look very sad."

"My radio's are not working, and today is the final game between India and Australia and I would love to hear the match. I might as well have gone to work with my diarrhea and upset stomach."

"Don't worry, Uncle," Sen assured. "I have my transistor radio. You can take it and listen to the commentary. I'll come and hear the score from you and that would be fine with me."

Sen was a sales representative for a pharmaceutical company. Appa and he were good friends, even though Sen was about twelve to fourteen years younger. Sen would also act as a doctor and bring free samples of medicines to him, much to my mother's mortification. Dad would gladly accept these pills and ointments and had no problem self-treating himself with these complimentary drugs. They were pretty benign pills like Tylenol and aspirin, with an occasional hemorrhoid cream and antifungal solution thrown in.

"Moham, please make extra for lunch, as Sen will join us for the same," he called out to my mother before she started to prepare for lunch.

Sen was Appa's hero when he gave him his transistor radio to listen to the day's match. The second inning began with Farooqh Engineer at one of the wickets. It was pin-drop silence except for the hum from the transistor. Dad was lying on the bed with the radio glued to his ear.

"Moham, Engineer has scored 24 runs. He's playing very well. I think we're going to win today."

"I'm glad your stomach and diarrhea have settled. What would you like for your lunch, now that we have Sen joining us?"

"Are you irritated that Sen is joining us for lunch?" my father asked guardedly.

"Of course not, it's just that you are not setting a good example to your children," she replied. "You know your daughters. Before long, they'll make excuses like what you did today and not go to school too." She was remembering the time my sister pulled a fast one on her about not being able to see so she could stay home.

"I don't think you have to worry about them," replied my father. "They have taken after you."

Sen came knocking at the door. "Hi, Uncle, how's our team doing?"

At that moment, Engineer was bowled out for a mere 29 runs and was the first wicket to fall for India. My father, visibly upset, conveyed the sad turn of events to Sen, who was being beckoned by his wife and could not linger. "That's disappointing," he waved as he left. "India has to face this crucial loss so early in the game. I'll be back soon."

"Moham, this Sen is a bad omen for the Indian cricket team. He just knocks on the door and asks for the score and a wicket is down," Appa speculated and complained about the sad turn of events to my mother.

"What is the matter with you? You have his transistor and he can't ask you for the score? Instead you call him a bad omen for just inquiring? This is as bad as the crow that came to sit on the palm tree and the coconut fell.

Let's not discuss about Sen. It's lunchtime and I've made a good vegetarian lunch for him and his wife."

The doorbell rang again, and what do you know? It was Sen. "Uncle, what's the score?" he asked Appa.

"Sen, please don't ask for the score. Do you hear what I hear?" He put the radio to Sen's ear. "We have tragically lost another wicket." This time it was Pataudi, the captain of the Indian team, who had scored a single run and not displayed any leadership throughout this game at the Eden Gardens in Calcutta. His first-inning score was only 15 and he barely lasted for a run. India was at a shaky 93 runs, showing all signs of losing to the stronger team. "I don't think the vibes from you are right," Appa said. "Every time you utter the word 'score,' somebody gets bowled out, man."

If I had been Sen, I would have grabbed my transistor radio from this old man's hands and walked out of his house, never to return. Out of the kindness of his heart, Sen gave up his time with his transistor to listen to a match commentary where cricket history was to be made. No! Sen deserved what he was getting from my father. He did not say boo to him. He quietly walked home, took some medication from his briefcase pharmacy, and returned to be subjected to some more insults.

"Uncle, I think your stomach must not feel good. These are the new charcoal tablets that can remove bloating caused by gas. This other medicine takes care of nausea and diarrhea. Take it," Sen gently coaxed my father as he sat next to him on the bed.

If there was one other thing that Appa loved other than cricket it was polypharmacy and self-treatment. Sen was the supplier of Aludrox, Unizyme, and milk of magnesia. His home pharmacy had drugs which would give Appa constipation, for which treatment was immediately available in another row where he had some laxatives. He manipulated his bowels masterfully with Sen's help, and I wonder if Appa was Sen's guinea pig outside of his company. I never saw Appa use any habit-forming medications; most of his meds were to help with nausea, hyperacidity, reflux, diarrhea, hemorrhoids, and headaches.

Immediately Appa and Sen were friends. They were now listening together to the score while my mother got the lunch ready. She joined the two to listen. This was her way of maintaining Appa's demeanor, which she would do successfully with her silent stare and nonverbal eye communication, should he repeat the offense about the "bad omen" nonsense if and when India lost another batsman.

India was losing badly to the visiting Australian team. For a mere 161 runs, India succumbed to the great bowling by the Australian spinners. The second inning was very quickly won by the opponents. They just needed to score less than 50 runs and they won the game with all ten wickets in their hands. If this game had been played in any other city in India, the city may have been spared. But this loss was in Calcutta, where the passionate cricket fans are sore losers. All streets were brought to a standstill and there was a riot initiated by the unruly fans. I was glad that Appa had not gone to work, as he may not have made it home that night. My mother had forgotten that Appa had taken a day off, and she was relieved to see that he was safe sprawled in bed in a *veshti* and an oxford shirt. Sen was lying down next to him munching on peanuts and trail mix that Amma had brought out for an afternoon snack. She and Sen's wife were watching these two men discussing the cricket matches as they decided on the dinner for the two families.

CHAPTER 10
Veshti with Vengeance

"Fashion is what you adopt when you don't know who you are."
                              Quentin Crisp

Veshti and Appa were synonymous. If I'd had a brother, he might have altered Appa's fashion sense. A wardrobe for a man from Madras consists of a *veshti;* an *angavastram,* a yard of cotton material strewn over the left shoulder; and a few white oxford shirts. He made a fashion statement when he woke up in the morning to take a shower and then adorned his body with stripes of *vibhuthi* (sacred ashes), wrapped the *veshti,* tossed an *angavastram* over his left shoulder, and off he went to work.

When he returned from work, the very first thing he did was wash his feet (and walk on the tiled floor tracking wet footprints), slip off his worn *veshti,* and don a fresh one. He was ready for the evening after his evening prayers. By the way, this was his makeshift pajamas too. Life was simple.

For a special day, such as a wedding, he would wear a *veshti* with a thicker border embroidered with gold motifs. It might be in cotton or in silk. As children, we were always awed by the way my mother wrapped her six yards of sari on her. For our small frames, it was easier to practice wearing a sari with Appa's *veshti,* as it was only four yards to wrap around us. We all practiced and messed his wardrobe of *veshti*.

When I was in fourth grade, I was chosen to act as one of the "six blind men of Hindustan." For those of you who are not familiar with this poem, it is about blind men giving their opinions of what an elephant looks like after feeling it, and here it is:

The Blind Men and the Elephant
by John Godfrey Saxe

It was six men of Hindustan
To learning much inclined,
Who went to see the Elephant
(Though all of them were blind)
That each by observation
Might satisfy the mind.
The First approached the Elephant
And happening to fall
Against his broad and sturdy side

At once began to bawl:
"Bless me, it seems the Elephant
Is very like a wall."
The Second, feeling of his tusk,
Cried, "Ho! What have we here
So very round and smooth and sharp?
To me 'tis mighty clear
This wonder of an Elephant
Is very like a spear."
The Third approached the animal,
And happening to take
The squirming trunk within his hands,
Then boldly up and spake:
"I see," quoth he, "the Elephant
Is very like a snake."
The Fourth reached out an eager hand,
And felt about the knee.
"What most this wondrous beast is like
Is mighty plain," quoth he;
"'Tis clear enough the Elephant
Is very like a tree!"
The Fifth, who chanced to touch the ear,
Said: "E'en the blindest man
Can tell what this resembles most;
Deny the fact who can,
This marvel of an Elephant

Is very like a fan!"
The Sixth no sooner had begun
About the beast to grope,
Than, seizing on the swinging tail
That fell within his scope,
"I see," quoth he, "the Elephant
Is very like a rope!"
And so these men of Hindustan
Disputed loud and long,
Each in his own opinion
Exceeding stiff and strong,
Though each was partly in the right
And all were in the wrong.

(from *wikisource.org*)

Amma and Appa, I got chosen to play the role of a blind man in a school play!" I rushed in to tell my parents. "I just can't wait for that day when the parents and the Catholic school priests and Mother Provincial will be visiting the school to see who should win the award for the play." I danced around the room excitedly. But then I was struck with a dilemma. "Mom, Cynthia and Joyce have brothers and they're going to wear their brothers' shorts and shirts. I won't fit into Dad's pants and shirt. What am I going to do?"

"Why, my dear, you are portraying a man from

Hindustan," Appa advised. "You should wrap a *veshti* for the play. What better way to see an Indian in a play?"

"I couldn't agree more," said Amma.

"I don't want to wear an old man's clothes. Have you ever seen anyone wear a *veshti* near my school? Even the gardener wears pants at my school, Appa. It's a Catholic school and they'll start to laugh if I go in one on stage."

"Sweetheart, you can't help it," Appa said. "You don't have any brothers to borrow their clothes. Your only other choice is to wear your skirt and blouse. How ridiculous that would be, if a man from Hindustan wore a dress!"

What possessed me to obey my parents, to this day I do not know. I did take the *veshti* to school. My teachers were absolutely thrilled and I was not. For the first time I wished I were one of those friends of mine playing the elephant, hidden under a mountain of white and gray bed covers disguised as the pachyderm in the sweltering heat. My five friends, dressed in shorts and shirts as blind men, consoled me. In my mind they were appropriately attired.

"Don't worry. We're blind anyway. We don't care what you wear."

But they could not stop from grinning as I was the first to enter the stage in Appa's *veshti* wrapped in the style of a *panchagachcham* (where the *veshti* is wrapped in between the legs). I had a turban to complete the outfit, and I sure brought a roar of laughter as I entered the stage to feel the elephant. My father was proudly watching me from the audience. You can guess who won the prize for realistic depiction of an Indian blind man. It was embarrassing for me to even have to go back on-stage to receive it.

We returned from the final day of school, as it was winter break. I helped my mother with the packing and we were all set for our famous trip to Madras on the Madras express. This time Appa was not going to be irresponsible, as my mother had given him an ultimatum. If he did any disappearing acts, then he was on his own. With no further discussions or drama for a household which was fueled by dramatics, we took off to the Howrah railway station. Dad had acquired a new habit, something that met with disapproval from one and all in the family and I had not tweaked into the reasons for my mother's melodramatic snubbing of my father.

It became evident in our train ride. As soon as we got into the train, we were all comfortably bundled up to go to sleep. Before long, day was breaking and the dawn over Orissa was outstanding. The train was rapidly moving toward Andhra Pradesh, the state north of Tamil Nadu state. This was where Appa had received his education in agriculture. I could see his enthusiasm as he sat next to me for the ride through his favorite state, where he'd realized freedom.

"Do you see the fields are flooded with water and the women are standing planting the paddy field? Paddies need flooding in order to grow and yield rice. These are some of the best paddy fields in the world, and India and China produce most of the rice for the world."

The train rolled over the Godavari River bridge and we all tossed in coins wishing for something. There must be a lot of coins in the riverbed, I mused. Once when we were going over the same bridge in the summertime, the river had dried and people were picking the coins.

The next station we came to was Waltair, where the train started to go in the reverse direction, and I started to cry that we were going back to Calcutta without visiting Madras. Appa explained the reason it was happening—that the train was changing gauge.

"Appa, is that a rice plant too that I see on this side of the train?"

"No, it's another plant, called tobacco," he said excitedly. "It's a plant that grows in the shade and is used in cigars, cigarettes, and snuff."

"You shouldn't be discussing this with a nine year old," my mother interjected, and I knew that this was the reason why she was shunning Dad. Dad was not smoking, but he had started to chew tobacco. My *chitthappa* Balu came to know of my father's new habit as soon as we landed at the Madras Central Station.

"Tsk tsk, what is this I see that you are doing, Ambi? Father is not going to be too pleased when he sees your yellow stained teeth and the smell of tobacco." He looked at Appa amusedly and shook his head disapprovingly. "With a father like ours, you sure have a lot of guts, I must say, Ambi."

"Balu, can you stop at the local pharmacy, where I can get some clove and mint-based chewing gum?" Appa requested. "I can hide the smell, and it will also stop me temporarily from needing a fix."

"Don't worry. I am there to stop any altercations with Father. Just don't smile for the next two weeks. Act serious and somber. You know how to act in front of Dad. He's as much an expert about you as you are about him."

"Hey, Balu, what's cooking with the old man?" Appa asked seriously. "Now that he's planning to retire, our lives at home need serious overhaul. I'll manage for two weeks. What about you?"

I was not missing a word. I was all ears whenever our families discussed dynamics between my uncles and aunts. Generally speaking, they rescued each other if any of them inadvertently slipped into the hot fire of wrath flamed by home politics.

"Father has mellowed," replied my uncle Balu. "He's aging, and I don't think we have to fear him. You're a father too. Let him know that. But, Ambi, you have to use some sparklers, man, to get rid of the brown coating on your choppers or else you'll be in serious trouble from the time you step into the front hall. What is it about you? Can't you go through life without a vice? Balram is right about you. He always said that you never fall into bad habits. Bad habits fall for you."

Appa started to grin from ear to ear. "Enough of teasing me. Tell me about your law practice."

"It's fine. But what do I see here? You've lost a tooth. How did that happen?" "I was playing cricket. The ball knocked my tooth off."

"That needs some major work. Let me take you to my friend, Dr. Giri. He may polish those teeth and let you even dare a smile in front of father."

Appa had fallen into a major unhealthy addiction for chewing tobacco. Now I could see why my mother was not pleased about any educational lessons about tobacco cultivation. This habit was hard to shake off, and only God knows that he tried many times and failed miserably. He would desperately take on to smoking before our trips to Madras so that his teeth did not stain from the chewing of tobacco. Eventually this was the plant that was going to wound him mortally. When he did hear about the cancer in his jaw, he never chewed another strand of tobacco. But it was too late and he knew it. He repented, and I know he wished that he had listened to his wife, brothers, and daughters. But none of us said 'I told you so,' as it was no use making him feel terrible about something that could not be changed. He had to bear the cross and he knew it.

CHAPTER 11
Artist Dad

> "The only time I feel alive is when I am painting."
>
> Vincent van Gogh

As a young man, when Appa lived at home with his parents, he got no encouragement to paint. Thatha looked at him with total disapproval, had no patience, and did not admire his artistic flair. Thatha let him know in no uncertain words that this would not put food on the table. Well, Thatha had forgotten that he himself had been doing a successful job of bringing home the bread by working in the movies.

If they had any disagreement, Appa stomped out of the house and took a bus to Mahabalipuram. There, he would spend days learning how to sculpt, and he created many stone carvings. But he never questioned Thatha's dislike for art and whispered in his mother's ear, "He's not leading by example, is he? He is working in the art field too." Appa enjoyed and improved his painting skills on the sly. Who had ever heard of a nice young lad disobeying his father in the 1930s and doing what he wanted to do passionately? Not in my grandfather's household. Appa never did show these art pieces to his father, for he knew that there would be no eulogy showered on him.

"Ambi, you are such a good artist," my grandmother supported him. "I know that your *appa* does not like you wasting time painting. But I like your work. I'm afraid that envious people will cast an evil eye on your work that is so beautiful." Yet she was also fearful of his father reprimanding him over his artwork. In addition, she was superstitious and believed that envy and jealousy were vile attributes that certain people projected onto others. Not much for display and personal promotion at an art exhibition, Appa went through his teenage years not sure as to what he should be. He acquired his bachelor's degree but continued to paint when he left home.

We three sisters were always amidst easels, wet paint, and canvases strewn all over our home. Artists materials spread around did not matter to any of us, come to think of it. I did not know otherwise. There was always a lot of excitement as soon as a blank canvas got prepared for painting, and we all eagerly waited for Appa to begin. My mother would get a little irritated by the mess it created; after all, she was the one who was left to clean up.

Relentless Brush Strokes

The elaborate preparation Appa did before his canvas was readied was memorable. Rarely did he go to buy canvas. Cardboard sheets were bought in bulk. His canvas was made from *veshtis* glued together by all-purpose-flour glue. The *veshti* that my dad once modeled was assuming a second life. This muslin cloth was cut into equal pieces, and Amma and Appa would have it layered between thick glue and left to dry for days in the sun. Once the material was firm like a canvas, it was prepared with gypsum and left to dry. The frames were handmade, the muslin *veshti* canvases were stretched onto them, and they were ready to be worked on. These canvases have withstood time, and the paintings are still beautiful.

With the first brushstroke, Appa would call for my mother: "Moham, I want some coffee."

"Be careful with your coffee. Keep it on a different table. Don't keep it so close to the cleaner and the linseed oil," she advised him.

"I'll remember," he replied absent-mindedly.

"Put away your clothes, books, and other valuables, as Appa has begun his painting," my mother alerted all of us. He could paint the canvas, but that did not deter him from cleaning the brush with my sari, even though rags had been provided for this purpose. He was so engrossed in his creation that the world came to a standstill as he painted a still life. There was many a time

I would complain to Amma about Appa having messed our beautiful outfits. He would try his level best to get the paint off our clothing, unsuccessfully. When he was in this creative mood, he would get up at all hours of the day and be absorbed in his artwork, oblivious to the world around him.

"Come for lunch," Amma called out to Appa.

"I will," he replied absent-mindedly, continuing with his relentless brushstrokes.

Half an hour later, "You have forgotten about your lunch," Amma reminded him. These calls from Amma during his creative days fell on deaf ears. I heard her monologues as Appa was not even responding to her calls to come for lunch or supper. "This is not good for your health. You have to stop at a convenient point and have your meals," she complained.

"I have not even finished the coffee and you are calling me for lunch." All the warning that my dad received about the cup of coffee had fallen on deaf ears. "The coffee is too cold. Could you reheat my coffee? Moham, the coffee does not taste the same. It's too weak."

Amma was exasperated. Here she was ready to serve lunch and Appa was still on his morning cup of coffee. She quickly went to see him before she had the lunch served.

"Well, I gave you a hot cup of freshly percolated coffee. If this is not good, we have to go and pick our own coffee from the plantation," she grumbled as she walked toward him to reheat the coffee. Then she froze in her tracks. "I just don't believe that you have done this!" she blasted my father angrily. She saw that the paintbrushes were in the coffee and that he must have taken a swig of the paint mixer.

"Now I know why the coffee didn't taste right," he smiled apologetically.

"You are coming with me for lunch," Amma commanded, visibly annoyed with Appa. "You are going to have your lunch and we won't bring coffee near your painting anymore. You could kill yourself if you drank one of those paint mixes."

Appa's other passion was to take us to the zoo or the botanical gardens. It was an experience. When I was young, I had a full dose of Latin words for animals, ordinary shrubs, and bushes. Not only did he carry his pad to draw the scenery and immortalize the day, he would be a walking encyclopedia of how to grow the flowers and take care of them. He was enthusiastic, curious, and interested in the nature that surrounded him.

"Look at this beautiful *pantheris tigris,* a powerful animal." Before long we were in the small animal section and we got to see the poisonous snakes, frogs, and toads. "Lalla, this is *rana tigerina,*" he pointed to the frog.

I had memorized the two Latin words and wanted to show off at school. "I saw the *rana panther*," I said proudly to Joyce, my best friend.

"The panther's name is Rana?"

"No, tigers are called *rana panthers*," I informed her. I had mixed up the Latin names for the tiger and a frog.

Appa's sisters were artists too. But he himself had created three daughters who did not display any artistic abilities. Our creative aspiration included a visit to an art gallery with Appa. You could see his mood change and his eyes brighten as he entered a different stratosphere. We would spend hours together loitering around the art gallery. We could never get bored as Appa was our guide for the grand visit. Before we knew it, we'd learned all you needed to know about an artist and how he'd created his artwork. Appa created three daughters in his life's art collection. We were all nerds like him, but we could not draw a straight line, even with some help from a ruler.

"Appa, I have a project. I have to paint a map of South America and draw the course of the river Amazon and paint the grasslands, the mountains, and rain forests." This was the geography homework I had brought home and was attempting to color. I showed him my work and he said, "You have really not done an accurate job. Let me help you." Before I knew it, he had done the whole painting. I do not know how many of you have fathers who love helping you with homework. Helping means to see you complete the job under their supervision. Not this time. He had seriously destroyed my homework by doing a fantastic display of the map of South America, which obviously to any eyes was not done by a child, or even by just any adult, but had been created by hands that belonged to an artist.

"Amma, can you see what Appa has done to my South America map? I can't take this to school. My teacher will never believe that I did this work." I burst out crying, as I did not have another map tracing to do my homework without Appa's help. I reluctantly took Appa's creation to school and handed it over to my teacher. I was embarrassed by the work that was not done by me but was too scared to tell my teacher anything, and I had a migraine from being in such a precarious position. Appa looked apologetic and just did not know how to undo his actions, as it was a watercolor work and indeed looked beautiful. "I'm sorry, I didn't mean to complete it, and I was trying to make it look childish. Let the teacher know that you promise to redo the homework without your *appa*'s help." He was truly sorry for what he had done.

"That's okay, Appa," I said. But who cared? This could not have been produced by an eleven year old, and so the map was returned to me by my teacher with the comment across the bottom of the map: "This is not your own work." I told my teacher what really happened and she let it go, but I was not about to excuse my father that easily. "The map was admired by the whole class for its workmanship, but who cares? 'THIS IS NOT YOUR OWN WORK,' " I confronted him. Amma told him off and I pouted around with my wounded ego.

I learned two lifetime lessons: You cannot shine in borrowed feathers; and you can try your best, but you do not have to be the best. You have to shine under your own lighting. That was the last time that we allowed Appa near any of our artwork. We did not do all that well, and we did not care, as one artist per home is plenty. "To take care of more than one artist in a home will require a school teacher's disciplinary hand," my mom said.

Appa would go into a shell if he did not get his dose of art. We could see that he got moody and snappy if his creative quality had not been put to action. Sometimes he just did not know what to paint. "Why don't you go to the art gallery or the museum, you may get stimulated," Amma would encourage. Many a time they would be at art shows, even though Amma did not have the same interest that Appa did. She would look at the artwork through his eyes and would be thrilled to see his enthusiasm.

Calcutta was having a large marble temple erected. We should have known that Appa would be part of the scenery. That whole year he had forgotten his family, friends, and job. He was busy sculpting the idols, painting them, and carving the beautiful elephants on the sides of the temple. His involvement at the temple was time consuming, and he had decided to quit his job.

"You didn't tell us that you quit your job?" Amma asked, furious about his decision. Who would not be? She found out when she called his workplace. My mother was livid. "You have three children. You are so irresponsible!" She complained bitterly and chastised him for his lack of accountability toward his family.

Appa was finally doing what he loved. He was close to attaining his nirvana through his art and was doing something for his soul, and here his family was complaining about him quitting his job. We did go to see his artwork at the temple. We were the prejudiced bunch, as Amma was displeased with Appa's conduct and callousness in having let go of a good job just to do sculpting at the upcoming temple.

Needless to say, Appa was back at home after completing his temple work, and now Thatha, who had gotten wind of Appa's deviation from engineer to artist, was even more irritated with his son. He immediately asked for him to return to Madras and assist with the dairy business at the farm. This needed help and who better than a man who had a degree in agriculture? We were taken care of in Calcutta, with Thatha making sure that we lacked nothing. My poor *Appa* lasted just a few months under his father's thumb.

If Picasso had a blue period that he portrayed, this was Appa's blue period, which he could not portray with his paints and brushes in Madras. So, without his paintbrushes to portray his misery, this was the letter he wrote to Amma:

> My dearest Moham,
> I cannot tell you how much I miss you and the children. Here, my life is worse than hell. Why do I have to obey my father and do what he wants to achieve? Whatever I do or don't do does not bring any approval from my father. I am his big disappointment and I am not about to stay with him and listen to this every day. I hate these cows and I don't care if they are milked or used for mowing the lawn. All I can think of is being with you. You have got to write to my father that your life without me is miserable and unbearable. Mine here is miserable and unbearable. He never leaves his wife to wander off anywhere. Why the hell does he expect me to leave my loving family to cater to his cows? I want to come home.

Please give my love to Lalitha, Prema, and Swathi.

I miss you a lot and I want to see you right now.

Yours affectionately

R. Swamy

As soon as we returned from school, we saw Amma crying inconsolably. "Mom, why are you crying?" I asked. Amma showed me the letter written by Appa to her.

"We have to do something for him," she said. "I cannot bear to see him this unhappy. He can't live without us four. I feel responsible for what is happening to him."

My sisters and I were now sure that Appa was not going to last in Madras without us. We gave a cock-and-bull story about how Amma needed him. We were not doing well at school without his help with our homework, and this was not good for us. So we immediately brought him back to Calcutta.

If I could describe a happy day in our family, it was the day that Appa arrived back from Madras. We wanted to keep him entertained after the rough time he'd had in Madras. The very next day we decided to take him to his favorite haunts, movies, and dinners on Park Street, so that he could block out his time in Madras. He was like a little child back to his old activities, and I don't believe he stayed home for long. He was off to work and my mother swore never to snitch on my father to his father. Appa may have spent six months of his life apart from Amma after their marriage. She called him her bad habit. For him, she was his soul, sole support. I did not notice this until I became a wife. He was dependent and she a dependable lady. He was the free spirit, while Amma was the force to let him explore. When broken by his weaknesses, Amma was his crutch that healed him. We children were excited to have our father back in our home.

CHAPTER 12
A Parent Apparent

> "Any man can be a father. It takes someone special to be a dad"
> -Author unknown

I never knew of Fathers Day until I came to Canada. I was awed by the greeting cards, coffee mugs, and T-shirts that were being sold to the poor children about to celebrate in praise of their father. The poor Western children have fallen prey to symbolize and pay tribute to a very special man for only one day of the year. What about the other days? We have heard the expression that anybody can be a father, but only few can be a dad. Some fathers fall into the crack, smack between being father and dad. As a child, I felt that there were days when Appa was a dad and there were days when he was just a father. I am sure that all children will agree that there is no dad in this universe who is a perpetual star performer.

I remember our servant, Beli-ka-ma (literal translation, "Beli's mother"), who was the single parent to her two children. She had a daughter named Beli who had been married off at the age of ten but returned to her mother's home because her husband abused her. Beli-ka-ma had been subjected to the same when she was young and had decided to walk away from the situation. She was now Beli-ka-ma-bap ("Beli's mother and father"). Raised by only her mother, Beli the daughter would come to our place with her mother to help with cleaning and washing. From time to time, Beli's father would return periodically into their lives to demand money and physically abuse them if the same was not given. He was the perfect example of a "deadbeat dad." He rose from being dead intermittently to do some beating. Here was a man who was not in the crack between father and dad but in a deep pit of castigation, never to recover. Beli and Beli-ka-ma left a lasting impression on my life. I may not call them friends, but they were special people in our household. I don't remember the day I got to know them, but I do remember that Beli-ka-ma was the first person who woke me up every day shouting in my ears, "Uttho Beti nehi tho School ke liye dher ho jayega!" (Wake up, my child, or else you will be late for school). She had a small mud house and would ask special permission from my parents to take us to her place to give us sweets on Diwali day. We loved visiting her place. She had a goat that gave her fresh milk, a dog that kept her place safe, and her home was clean. We could play around with her goat, dog, and children.

When we make new friends, we remember the first day we meet them. I tried to rewind my memory tape to remember the very first day of such a meeting between my parents and me. This is a very difficult exercise. They have been there with you right from the very first time that you let out the first cry of attention. Anyway, I thought it was a useful exercise, and I for one do not remember any of the days that I was being carried around by Appa when I was a year old, or for that matter when I was two years old. The very first day that I can visualize in my memory video was when I sat on his lap with a banana in my hand. The banana was in exchange for a complete shaving of my head. That is my very first recollection of him. He was holding me still while in a religious ceremony my first baby hair was given to a God. This is an ancient ritual and is still carried out. For my kids we had to modify this procedure and offered a lock of hair at the local temple. This ceremony hopes to fulfill your dreams and wishes for the child. I did not understand the connection between the hair and the underlying benefit reaped by this performance. But who was I to question an ancient ritual at the age of three? I can still visualize the scene. Cold water was drawn from the well at the temple and poured over my shaved head. I screamed and threw a tantrum on Appa's lap. That was the very first day that I met him.

I guess this hair offering ritual has left an everlasting impression in me. I had long, flowing hair all the way to by waist. When it showed signs of thinning from stress, sickness, or the mere fact that one-half of my family was follicle challenged, I followed instructions from my aunt that the way to abort this process of youth alopecia was to offer the falling hair to Lord Venkateshwara at the temple in Tirupati. What do you know?—not a strand was left on the floor. All fallen tresses were collected, and anybody making the trip would take it to drop it off in Tirupati. I did not realize that these hair offerings were used to make wigs and extensions. The proceeds were used to set up schools and other forms of charities. I believe that Indian hair is popular for making wigs, as it is somewhere in between coarse and very fine hair, and the strands withstand several shampoos and brushings without losing sheen. Anyway, it went for a good cause. But, when I left India, my mother said that Appa came upon this large bag of hair and he could not believe that he had raised this silly daughter who would give in to such blind beliefs.

"All she needs is a good dose of vitamins and a less stressful life," he advised my mother. "She hasn't learned the art of relaxation from me. She should take up a hobby. She should stop being a doctor when she comes home. Moham, our children are 75 percent you and 25 percent me. They have not gotten the art gene from me. I wish that these children of mine could paint. They would never be lonely, stressed, or lack insight in life."

Our father-daughter time did not prepare me with paintbrush and canvas, but he sure taught me all I needed to appreciate a good painting when I saw one. We children were great at knowing the era an artwork belonged to. We also had a good inkling as to whether it was Realism, Impressionism, or Modern art. The small detail missing from these Appa-made art lover children was the skill to paint.

In India when I was growing up, creativity and art was not a major part of our curriculum. So my sisters and I again lost out on honing our artistic endeavors. But I did realize that the Catholic school I went to in Calcutta was like any school anywhere in the world. The only difference was that we did not have structured parent-teacher meeting days. Well, this did not mean we kids were free to do what we liked. My parents believed that every day was a parent-teacher meeting. Amma would come to pick us up from school every day. She always stopped to ask the teachers if we were doing well and if there was any subject that we should improve and needed coaching in. Can you believe this?—day after day your mother badgering your class teacher if there had been progress in her child within the eight hours of school attendance. Appa believed that his garden of children got their genetic fertilization at conception and that you were born an artist or not, born to be a genius or not. He did not believe that the seven hours were going to transform his imps into anything. So, he showed up once a month to torment our teachers. No other kids at school had their parents dropping in and contacting their teachers as frequently as ours did. I even confronted my parents on this issue.

"Why do you have to talk to my teachers every day? So I came third instead of first in arithmetic. Joyce is better than me. I can't help it."

"Well, you can't do poorly at school," Mom insisted. "Your *Appa* won't like you getting low grades. He's going to be upset."

Was she really referring to *our Appa*? He could never get angry at our mediocre grades. Disciplining us over grades was not his style. Was Mom talking about our neighbors' reaction to their son's grades? Or she must be talking about Thatha and not about Appa. First of all, he did not even keep tabs on which grade we girls were in. Second of all, he'd had enough of being under the eagle eyes of discipline and being reprimanded. He had other plans for his children. He would never question us if we

Relentless Brush Strokes

did poorly, and if Amma prodded him to do so anyway, he would not be able to do it with a straight face.

"Let the children be children. They have all their lives to be responsible," Appa would whisper to her.

Amma knew that it was she who had issues with our grades and not Appa. The two of them balanced out to be great parents. We could slip out of our ever loving mother's discipline-bound arms easily into our more than easygoing playful father's arms.

Some days, both of our parents came to the school to pick us up. When we were young and embarrassed about being under the watchful eyes of our parents, it felt like it happened too frequently, but now my mother recalls it to be a rare occurrence—our parents together at our school waiting in the front school yard, where we three sisters wanted to disappear from the face of the earth. The closing school day assembly would be over, we would be lined up outside the classrooms, and our friends would point to our parents on the lawn. Our parents were not just visiting the school to pick us up, they were not just sitting on a bench in front of the school, they were actually sprawled under the mango tree with eyes only for each other. Not that they were a romantic couple fit to be in a Bollywood movie, but who wants to see their parents display any form of public affection? By the way, they were not holding hands, touching, hugging, or kissing.

But as we know in Bollywood, none of these acts need to be done to be deemed romantic, as we Indians believe in a higher form of love, i.e., cosmic love. It is a spiritual love affair where we fantasize bodily union. Believe it or not, we children, so used to seeing Bollywood movies, thought my parents were playing a scene from a movie under the mango tree. My younger sister was embarrassed, came up to me, and said, "You are the oldest. You've got to tell them not to show up at school. All my friends are teasing me that they're 'in love.' How can I show my face to my friends? Their parents don't do this."

Our school principal Sister Elizabeth always chuckled to herself when she saw the two lovebirds under the mango tree. She would come to me and say, "Your mom is well endowed and your father is lean. She doesn't feed him enough." I really did not need any description of my parents' physical attributes when I was already embarrassed from their public display of affection. Anyway, my dad and mom would saunter up to make small talk with my principal about their three precious children.

Sister Elizabeth had a soft spot for our family, and I visited her when she was old and had retired into St. Vincent's Home. She had some stomach problems, for which I prescribed her some medication. She reminisced about school days, my parents, and the great time she had being a school principal.

Relentless Brush Strokes

Appa's religious preferences did not stop him from sending his children to a Catholic school. The Christian missionary schools were considered to be the best, and it was difficult to procure admission to them unless you were a Christian or were willing to pay big school fees. But he had two good friends in Father Rajan and Brother Joseph, with whom he shared religious forums and compared Hinduism with Christianity. This was to our advantage, and his three daughters were packed off to a great school for a song.

We would learn Catholicism at school, come home, and carry on reciting our hymns while Appa continued to chant his Sanskrit prayers as a practicing Hindu. Our friends outside of school largely consisted of Muslims, Catholics, and Hindus. Appa was a tolerant Hindu and enjoyed Christmas with his Catholic and Hindu friends. Our home was the place of congregation for all our family's and friends on Christmas day.

Calcutta is a cosmopolitan city with a large Christian population. Christmas is not taken lightly in Calcutta. Furthermore, Appa loved Christmastime. Dad was no longer seen in his *veshti* and *angavastram*. He had metamorphosed into a full-blown Westerner in a suit and tie. He was ready to serve scotch on ice and Johnnie Walker whisky to everyone. He loved to play host around this time. We had forgotten that we were Hindus and we seemed to be enjoying the Christmas carols, fruit cakes, and other goodies. Our Catholic friends were ready to go to Mass, and we were dressed to attend the church. Appa loved getting our home ready for the party at which he was to play host, enjoying his occasional beer, whisky, or scotch. Just a small problem: These drinks did not love my dad. One drink he could tolerate; the next drink, we would all think he was coasting; and the third drink, he was out flat. The way we would deal with this when there was a big gathering was to let my uncle take over the bar to micromanage the titrated drinks that could be instilled in my father without losing him for the night.

CHAPTER 13
Literary Lot

> (In Sanskrit)
> Asato ma satgamaya
> Tamaso ma jyotirgamaya
> Mrtyorma amratam gamaya
>
> Lead me from the falsehood to truth
> Lead me from darkness to light
> Lead me from death to immortality
> —Brthadaranyaka Upanishad

Fridays and Saturdays were packed with literary action. As children, I and my sisters gave my mother some peace and quiet when Appa took us to the National Library in Calcutta. It is the oldest and the largest library in India. Located in the most serene, beautiful, and prestigious part of Calcutta called Belvedere Estates, it boasted a collection of rare books that put even Europe to shame. It was constructed in 1836, and the British played a large role in maintaining the place. Donations from various governor-generals in West Bengal contributed to this library, and it was only in 1953 that it opened to the general public. It was a fifteen-minute walk from our home, and we would take this stroll together.

"We are going to the library, do you want to come with us?" I asked my friends. No television or Gameboys for entertainment—we as children were content with simple activity, like just visiting the library. I don't remember if I could convince my children to take the stroll with me to the local library every week. The only time my children went to the local library was when they had some projects to do and they needed to do a literature search. Today TV and the Internet have stolen the joy from library visits.

The National Library had a beautiful children's hall and corner. Large doors led to the garden on the side, where there were chairs and tables for children to be seated while they read the library books. This was a treat for any child. You did not have to be a nerd to visit this library. Those were the days of Enid Blyton storytelling, and we slowly graduated from "Noddy" tales to the "Circus Day" series and then to all her school serials. Our book reading habits were fostered by my father. He would leave us in the childrens section and take off to the larger adult section. After two to three hours at the library, we were treated to ice cream on our way home.

We visited a lending library with Appa to bring back several books and read them as if there was no tomorrow.

My favorite recollection of him was lying down by his side and reading the same book together with him. We would be on different pages in the same book. He would turn the pages as we would snuggle up to him under the blanket. "I am going to give out the mystery if you do not hurry up," he teased us, as he was ahead by a page. This he did with his three daughters and enjoyed brain time with us. We were the best of friends when it came to reading. The discussions that would ensue from these readings could go on for days. Any book considered to be a classic would be bought and added to our book shelves.

Appa hated parting with his books. If he did loan a book, I would not be surprised if he did not mark it with his blood. If he let anyone borrow his books, he would remember them and constantly remind the individual that the book has not been returned. My cousin became an unforgettable culprit. He had borrowed Ayn Rand's *Atlas Shrugged,* and, Appa met him ten years later in Toronto. As Appa shook his hands, he did not say, "How are you?" Instead, he questioned, "Where is my *Atlas Shrugged?*" According to our Hindu culture, you never borrow. For if you do, and do not return it in this life, you will be punished and reincarnated as a slave or in some other subservient form to pay your dues back to the one you borrowed from. As Appa believed in reincarnation and karma and so on, he held my poor cousin responsible for returning this valuable piece of literature to him in this life, or he was doomed, as Appa might haunt him in the next life still asking for his *Atlas Shrugged*.

Passionate about reading, he even taught me a simple experiment called the "power of the printed word." He painted a yellow square and wrote inside the square "Red," and inside a painted red square he wrote the word "Green," and so on. He then asked me to quickly tell him what colors the squares were in order, and I read the words instead of describing the correct colors of the squares. He then smiled and explained to me that my error was because the printed word had more power and ruled the brain.

He had no time for the ignorant. He assumed that the ignorant did not try and that all was available for one to be enlightened. He was a strong believer in "what the mind does not know, the eyes do not see." He took this saying to a different level, especially if he met someone with whom he could not even discuss an interesting piece of literature. He would comment, "How will a donkey know the aroma from camphor?" He felt that all your faculties and senses were dulled and not receptive if you did not hone your brain with printed matter. He would tell us that the only asset that parents should leave for their children is the gift of *Saraswathi* (God of knowledge). "No one can rob your knowledge away from you. You can impart this knowledge only through teaching others. All materialistic wealth can be easily lost, but education allows for you to be independent."

When Appa was visiting Los Angelas, his library-going habits were not over and done. "The library is getting rid of some of its old books," he called my sister Swathi. "Bring three or four large garbage bags. The librarian told me that we are allowed to take as many books as possible for $10, but we cannot return for more." He had it clarified by the librarian whether he was allowed to carry out only as many as his arms could hold or could use other means. Well, who was to stop this enthusiastic reader and his progeny Swathi? Three garbage bags of all kinds of prints in any subject that he and my sister fancied were dragged out for $10 by my book-crazed family.

Appa could be the cool dude and read comics and current best sellers to discuss anything with our friends who visited us. This, of course, would annoy us, as we did not want him hanging around our friends. I complained to Amma that he was annoying me. Couldn't she ask him to take a hike and stop annoying my friends with all the interesting things that he read or saw? Amma would quietly use sign language to beg of him to leave the kids alone. We thought our friends were talking to Appa out of respect. I was fortunate enough to meet one such friend of mine who used to stop by my place almost every day.

I was under the misconception that he came over just to meet me. Later on I found out that our friends were truly interested in Appa's teachings on spirituality and philosophy. I never gave any credit to Appa for being a cool dad.

As a matter of fact, both my parents were considered to be cool. Young and old came to see them with their problems and issues. Our family home was the harbinger for many activities in which Amma and Appa gave advice to the youngsters. Some families that had children deviating from traditional ways also came to my parents for help. It was on one of these trips to the local lending library that we stopped at the stamps museum. We went in to discover that there was more to learn from these small printed postages than just using them to send mail. He got me and my friends all interested in collecting stamps.

"Lalla, you get the red album; and Prema, you get the smaller blue one; and Swathi, you are the baby and you deserve the baby album." He cheerfully bought us all our very own stamp albums.

"Appa, how do I stick the stamps onto the pages?"

"We'll first sort the stamps according to the country. All of the stamps have to be categorized according to the date they've been published, or you can sort them according to flowers, animals, etc."

"Appa, I have two of the same kind," I announced.

"No problem. You give your duplicate to your sister and in return ask her for another one. She may have two of another kind and you may not have it." If baseball cards were being traded in America, in Calcutta we were busy trading stamps.

We all had our own little albums organized, and Saturdays and Sundays were set aside to browse through them. We learned all that we needed to know about a country. Sometimes he had us collecting using a theme. All my friends were involved in it too. I still hold on to the prized possession. When I am old, I will look at this collection more somberly.

CHAPTER 14
Mantras and Vedas

Appa, I believe, had a dual personality. Even though he was God-fearing and did his prayers and continued to do what he considered was good, his deviation from being normal included collecting literature, especially if it was not available in the local bookstores. One such banned book was hidden away from all of us, Somerset Maugham's *Lady Chatterley's Lover*. His curiosity to find out more about such works got us into big trouble with Amma. Prema was engrossed in this book, which was covered from view by her school textbook. She was reprimanded and grounded for the same, as I could not help but squeal on her deviant behavior. Needless to say, the Upanishads, Gita, and Puranas were books and words that we grew up with. This did not mean that our home was harbored under a religious cult, nor were we staunch Hindus. Our book collection included Somerset Maugham's *The Razor's Edge,* Dennis Wheatley's books, Pearl S. Buck's stories from China, and Graham Greene's entire collection, among others. Amma belonged to the theosophical society, and her belief in religious activities was different from Appa's. Living in India sprinkled a good dose of Catholicism, Islam, Judaism, and Buddhism into our lives.

"Moham, the *dhobi* (washer man) has stained the *veshti*," Appa complained. For Veda chanting at Shankara Bhavan, he would be clad in a *dhoti* or *veshti*. If you look it up in Webster's Dictionary, a *dhoti* is "a loin cloth worn by men in certain parts of India." It was made famous to the world by Mahatma Gandhi when he attended the Round Table Conference in London and was called by Sir Winston Churchill a "half-naked Indian fakir [beggar]." A *veshti* as it is referred to in Tamil is about four yards of thin muslin or silk material with an embroidered cotton or gold border. It is worn with a *kurta* or simply a shirt. But my slight *Appa* wore this with an *angavastram* (a body cloth) that he tossed over his left shoulder. He adorned his body with three stripes of *vibhuthi*, or ashes on his forehead, arms, and forearms; and a small red dot on his forehead. He had his *poonal*, a sacred thread, across his shoulder; and it did not matter how cold it was, my father would display his God-fearing body to the public and was never bashful. Although he was an avid movie buff, he did not display any tendency to emulate Gregory Peck or Rock Hudson in his day-to-day living.

Relentless Brush Strokes

I thought Appa was cute, though I don't believe he was a Rock Hudson for looks.

"I'll talk to him about messing your *veshti,*" Amma placated him. "Just change. I don't want you to go to Shankara Bhavan wearing a stained one." If Amma did not prod him to change, he would not think it necessary to do so.

He would canter off to the local Shankara Bhavan to listen to some of the religious dissertations by prominent speakers. They would also chant the Vedas. Women did not attend these meetings, and Appa did not ask Amma to accompany him, even though she would have prepared the *prasaadam,* the offering to God, for all the men who attended this prayer meeting.

I was always embarrassed by the public display of Appa's bare-chested ash-striped body. I would cross the road and walk on the other side if I saw him in this form walking to his Veda classes on a Sunday evening. I thank Calcutta for its "load shedding" days, when the city had times when the electricity for a whole neighborhood was cut and it was in darkness. With this cyclical quota of a power supply and temporary darkness, we suffered from the stifling heat and no electricity; it was a blessing, though, as I could dodge from my father's religious outward appearance. This invariably happened in the hot summer days when the heat was unbearable and the electricity supply was a major problem throughout the city.

"Didn't you see Appa?" my mother asked me. "He's on his way to Veda classes."

"Amma, I saw the stark white fluorescent light stripes in this body bobble away in the dark," I joked. "His dark, unclad body with its ash stripes was visible in the darkness, and I thought it must be Appa!"

The *dhoti* is one of the oldest outfits known to mankind. It is at least 3000 years old, and I am sure that the material, the ease with which one can wear it, and the comfort it provides in the hot summer months are the reasons that to this day it is popular in India. It is as daily a comfort wear to Indians as jeans are to Americans.

Appa would spend weeks at the Shankar Bhavan and Veda Bhavan. He had all the sculptures in these two buildings resurfaced, refinished, and painted. The two buildings were closed temporarily when my father tirelessly worked in them, never complaining. The opening day was a great event, and my father was honored for the great work at the inauguration ceremony.

Appa and Amma were on their way to Canada and the United States to visit their daughters. "Moham, Singapore is like India. Everyone I have seen leaving for Singapore is dressed in a *veshti*. As we are traveling by Singapore Airlines, I will be more comfortable if I went in my *veshti*," Appa related his dress code to Amma. My dad did not believe in "when in Rome, do as Romans do." The Singapore flight was to land in Los Angeles.

"I want you to change in Singapore before we take off for LA," my mother told him. "Los Angeles is not like Singapore or India. We have been there before, and you should change into your pants. Even Mahatma Gandhi was not treated with respect when he visited England in this *dhoti*."

"I am comfortable for the long trip in my *veshti*, and I will change just before we land in Los Angeles," Appa assured her. But, lo and behold, the two of them forgot, and Mom did not remind my dad. Appa landed in Los Angeles in his *veshti*.

His granddaughter screamed with excitement when she saw her grandfather exit the plane. "Look, Mom, Thatha is wearing a tablecloth!"

My sister Swathi, like me, wanted to disappear from the face of the earth when she saw her dad at the airport. "Appa, there's a place and time to wear a *veshti*. This is not India. Why couldn't you have changed?"

"Forget it, *yaar*. This looks a lot more decent than the shorts and T-shirts that some of these men are wearing. Do you want me to show my legs?" he asked her jokingly.

Dhoti dramas took place in various parts of the continent, and none of us were immune to them, as my dad's favorite attire was a *dhoti*. When we had friends visiting us, I warned my dad that he should change and get ready for the visitors. If they were Indian friends, I might have excused him and let him model and prance around in his *dhoti*. But these were Canadians, and they were coming to meet with my parents for the first time.

Our friends arrived. It was a hot and humid summer day, and one of my friends, almost a foot taller than my slight dad, came in a tank top and shorts. About 80 percent of her body was unclad to keep her cool on this hot and humid day. On the other hand, my dad was sent off to change from his comfort clothing's—a *dhoti* and *angavastram*— to dress up in a pair of trousers and shirt, as he did not believe in wearing shorts and T-shirts.

Appa came down, saw my friend in her tank top, and whispered into my mother's ear, "Did you see the way this lady has arrived today? I have to cover all of my body on this hot summer day to socialize with this lady, who is happily exposing herself. I don't know where the logic to my dressing up lies." Come to think of it, why could he not have shown off his bare chest and wear a *dhoti* and *angavastram*? What skin off my nose was it? He was a proud Indian and he was not nude. He was respectfully attired. But there lay the difference between his free spirit and my inhibited ways.

Swathi had a big problem with gophers in her backyard when Appa was visiting her in LA. These rodents dug her whole garden up and were no longer lean animals. I had a glimpse at one of these in her backyard. They had chewed up her grass and eaten all her bulbs, and what was more, they were still coming back for more. My sister, who hated the gophers digging up her backyard, gave my dad the job of catching these pests, as she did not want to kill them.

"Appa, please get rid of these gophers. But don't kill them," she said. "Take them far away from our house and release them in the local park."

Appa had caught some in a big bag. "Swathi, I have caught some gophers, and I am going over to the park," he announced. "I'll be back soon."

"Appa, where are you going in your *veshti*?" my sister caught him red-handed walking across the street, but, of course, in his *dhoti*. "Please change into your pants, Appa." And so he changed before he took the gophers to the park. Dad was always dictated to when it came to his *dhoti*.

"Do you know something, Moham," Appa commented to my mother, "I have to change into trousers to drop these animals off in the park, and what do you know?—by the time I come and change again into my *veshti*, these bloody animals have dug their way back into our backyard and I have to get ready to don my pants to drop them again in the park. If this will please my daughter, I will do so and wear a tie too in honor of these critters!" He never did have any false pretenses, and this is just an example of the degree to which we would push him to change his ways and put on a facade for the public.

Appa enjoyed displaying his religious inspirations and loved to do exhaustive chanting of his mantras. I would tell him to say them softly. He, on the other hand, believed that even if you were not interested in what was being chanted, just hearing a prayer would make you spiritual, and someday by having heard it repeatedly you may chant on your own accord.

By Jove! Appa was right. I did not realize how much I knew until I was at the local temple in Toronto, where I heard the Vedas being chanted. I joined them. He had taught me.

CHAPTER 15
Arranged Marriages by Swamy

> I was married by a judge. I should have asked for a jury.
> —Groucho Marx

My mother's cousin, who was visiting us, was old enough to be married but had had no luck finding a mate. I do not believe that he even had any concept of finding his own bride. For some reason, much against what the Bollywood movies were trying to show to the general public, the men I knew when I was young were not acting boldly and picking up dates, as is very common amongst Western families. Needless to say, my mother's cousin was one more of those bachelors eagerly looking up to my parents to choose him a bride.

What do you know? Appa's friend and neighbor had his cousin visiting him from Patna at the same time. She was twenty-five years old and had parents who were eager to see her settle down with a nice man. Well, who better than my mother's cousin? Marriages may be made in heaven, but arrangements may have to be at the Swamys' residence. It was not an ordinary affair of just popping in and the cousins of the two families go out on a date. This would have been frowned upon by one and all, and most people in the sixties would have held the Swamys' responsible for such an aberrant act. Our family orchestrated a grand affair, with lavish provision of fruits, nuts, flowers, etc. These were all arranged in beautiful silver plates and were taken over to our neighbors' house. It would have been simpler if the families had let the two go out to a restaurant and get to know each other. No! Never! The chaperones who accompanied the prospective groom included my parents, my sisters, and I. For moral support, my mother's brother and his wife and family and good friends of the family from Ballygunge accompanied us. It was a daunting fourteen-member entourage that set off to pay a visit at our neighbor's. Well, our neighbors were not taking this *Penn pakkal* ceremony of checking out the prospective mate lightly either. They had their extended family and friends all eagerly waiting for us to show up at their doorstep. If only Groucho Marx had been born in India; he could have gotten a jury before the judge.

We were all dressed in our best silk outfits, and Appa had decided to color his graying sideburns. He wore his nice suit and tie and even put on some calamine cream, talcum powder, and aftershave cologne. He looked

Relentless Brush Strokes

handsome and smelled good too. I held his hand and followed the group to our neighbor's house.

The poor bride-to-be had her own nervousness to deal with. She wore a beautiful purple sari and matching flowers in her hair. She did not come out to greet us. As soon as we all settled in their living room, appetizers and coffee were brought for all of us. Tradition calls for the coveted girl to show up with the drinks and serve. This was the time when the prospective-groom's party would watch her walk and smile and listen to her talk. If her physical attributes fell short, then they would be civil and not feast on the goodies brought in by her. They would wait for the cue from the groom-to-be. If he seemed interested in pursuing this alliance, then conceding eye signals would be exchanged, and all of us would follow the vibes and the story might have a good ending.

My mother's cousin seemed interested when this beautiful lady walked into the room. She looked bashful and did not really pay much attention to the big crowd of people. She may have taken some side glimpses at my mother's cousin. Who knows? I did not see anything apparent between the two; I was twelve years old and did not know what exactly transpires when there is physical attraction. Now I can write a chapter on what can ensue from the interaction of estrogen and testosterone.

"Well, what do you think of her?" asked Appa.

"She's not bad looking," replied my mother's cousin. He was quite pleased with the girl and said as much to my mother.

After about an hour or two, we returned home. We were all excitedly discussing the day's event, and my mother and her brother were even planning for the upcoming wedding for their cousin. It was my mother who could not wait to hear what the girl thought of her cousin. So, off she went to our neighbor's house to find out the reaction from the girl.

"What did Buma think of my cousin?"

"I think she liked him," replied my mother's friend. "Can you wait? You may want to hear it from her. It's better than me trying to tell you what she felt."

"Hello, Buma," my mother greeted her cheerfully. After all, her cousin liked her, and it appeared that the feeling was mutual. Soon there would be wedding bells and Buma would be a relative.

"I hear that you liked my cousin," my mother enthused.

"He seemed like a nice man," replied Buma eagerly. "I was too shy to stare at him. But I did take a glimpse at him. He was looking at me through his glasses as he smiled at me."

My mother returned as quickly as she'd gone—visibly upset with Appa. "I cannot believe that on a day when we are trying to seek a bride for my cousin you would dress in your best and color your sideburns!" She ranted and raved about how ill-becoming his looks were, for he had not acted his age, especially when we were venturing out to look for a bride for someone. None of us understood why my mother was so upset with my father.

"What's the problem, Moham?" Appa asked, as he could not even comprehend my mother's wrath.

"Well, Buma, I believe, did not even cast a glance toward my cousin. She only saw you, and she tells me that she is willing to marry you!" My mother's cousin did not wear glasses, and no one wore glasses except Appa!

"She wants to see my cousin again," Amma sounded exasperated with Appa. She tried to coax her cousin to return to our neighbor's. Now her cousin was not interested in going back there to flaunt his looks. She and the neighbor apologized for the genuine mistake and were hoping that he would return so that Buma could take a second glance at the right person.

Poor Buma! An entourage of men had arrived for the *Penn pakkal* event, where she was to have focused on *the* man. How could she have differentiated? The poor girl had not even been officially introduced to him. She had just chosen the best-looking guy in the group—who happened to be none other than Appa.

Swayamvara is an age-old traditional way of choosing a life's partner by a woman, in which her parents line up all suitable grooms and she chooses one. No such luck when I grew up. I was born in the wrong era. Well, my mother's cousin was pissed off that he had not been noteworthy in the first place and that a married man had stolen his show.

We children were having the time of our lives when we heard that Appa had succeeded in the marriage arena without even making an effort. But that was not by my mother's viewpoint. She felt that he had overdone himself to look attractive when it had not been necessary. Needless to say, Appa was gloating, as he still had "it" after all these years. He continued to tease my mother about how he could easily find another woman.

Appa and Amma worked as a team to get my mother's cousin hitched, and they eventually succeeded. I decided even at a very young age that I was not about to let my parents tinker with my marriage. After all, Bollywood movies would slowly educate the general public and my parents and would someday change their views on arranged marriage as a whole. Even today, arranged marriages are not an uncommon occurrence. They are not unique to India. They happen in Iran, Pakistan, and Afghanistan and happened in Europe in the Victorian days. We can blame the British for introducing non-arranged marriage. I don't believe that the antithesis of arranged marriage is love marriage. That would be like saying that all Indian arranged marriages are without love. I for one had the experience of seeing my parents, who had had an arranged marriage. There had been a lot of care and love between those two.

I also would like to think that *all* marriages are arranged—by family or close friends who introduce single people to each other in a bar, at a bus stop, etc., which leads to an arrangement by the attracted parties to meet another day to explore a future. If to define an "arranged marriage" as one that starts with no love, then it would be appropriate to redefine love marriage as one with no arrangements. A love marriage without provisions might as well look outside for external help to rearrange the marriage agreements; for arranged marriages are successfully teaming and steaming and before you know it, the differences in the couple have been ironed out and they are prepared to work at this arrangement.

I am experienced in this department, as I have seen my parents make an arranged marriage work. One has to approach the living arrangements with utmost tolerance; and in my parents' case, my mother's tolerance was tested to its maximum. The engine in an arranged marriage is fueled by hopes to make it work, with no expectations from each other. The nonarranged marriage is fueled by passion and the certainty that "we know we are made for each other, so we have no problems." This can backfire if the couple does not give in to each other's idiosyncrasies. My mother gave in to my father's moods, tempers, and easygoing nature with level-headedness and equanimity. What I am trying to say is that whether a marriage is arranged or not, one should be ready to be pliable and accepting of whatever is about to happen or else it is bound to fail.

Another reason that it prevails in India is the social division created by the working class and the religious sects, which foster such arrangements made by their families. Most try to stick to their religious sects and social class. This is changing, as women are getting their university education and can find their own mates. Marriage and friendship are like a meadow, which needs attention and love. Without water, the fresh green lawn will become dry sod.

"Arranged marriage is for the birds," said my sister to me. "The Indians believe that a man is born somewhere for every woman. As you can see, homosexuality and gay culture has not even scratched our thought process. Otherwise the saying would be 'there is someone for everyone'."

Anjali, our neighbor, waited for that someone, and she was hoping against hope that her parents would be able to bring home a man for her, after thirty-three years of waiting and no luck from matchmakers and families. With her biological clock reminding her of lost days, she finally took the bait and eloped with our neighbor's son, Ahmed. Anjali had a double-edged sword to deal with. Not only did she marry in an unarranged way, but she went and married a Muslim. She hid from society and finally emerged when she needed to rearrange her life, with her pregnancy. She did return to Calcutta when she got pregnant, and her parents would not have anything to do with her. My parents were keeping a close watch on this poor girl and her antenatal care and delivery. After her child was born, Anjali and Ahmed's love story had a happy ending, and their parents made up with them, thanks to my parents.

The arranged marriages in our family were soon the forte of Appa's sister Athai. She networked with families who had boys and girls of marriageable age and had their hopes to marry tweaked by their horoscopes. The ultimate matchmaker, Athai brought in *varans* (men or women of marriageable age). She would match appropriate girls' and boys' horoscopes and let them know that this was a match made in heaven and that it was up to them to contact the families and get the *Penn pakkal* organized. Believe it or not, I have yet to see any of her matches failing. Appa did not believe everything she said, but she was my mother's best friend and confidante. All of our horoscopes are with her, and she not only predicted who we would marry, but also let us know about our unborn children, how wealthy or happy we would be, and so on.

Appa and Amma had a ready made "find your mate" advisor. Before long, she had roped in all three of us. She knew all of our in-laws before we knew them, and they worked hand-in-glove with her.

Indian society still offers arranged marriages. Websites like Shaadhi.com and Myindianmate.com are just a few that boast a large selection of men and women, where without the parents' watchful eyes they can assess each others' physical attributes and interests. But I believe that these cautious men and women still expect their parents to do the search and then give them a list of names to scout out. Athai has a busy practice, where making alliance is still not a thing of the past I gather. She will not accept money or gifts for the marriage-alliance advice she gives to her family and friends. I heard one Indian woman remark to her, "Who is better than your mother or father to choose your life's partner?" Her children were all rolling their eyes.

I am not about to find a husband for my girls. If I even chose a T-shirt for my daughters, they would exchange it or return it to me. Can you imagine the number of prospective men that may be arriving back at my doorstep? I let my daughters know that I am leaving all arrangements to them, and I am sure that love in both arranged and nonarranged marriages is a frequent occurrence. Marriage is a gamble, and there is a 50 percent chance that it may fail whether one chooses a partner or a partner is chosen for you.

I saw my girls sigh with relief.

CHAPTER 16
Father's Famous Festival

> Devout men (Yogins) who are intent (thereon) see this (spirit) seated in themselves; but the senseless, whose minds are unformed, see it not.
> —Bhagavad Gita 15:11

The principle motives behind most festivities in India are religious celebrations to mark an important beginning to a Hindu God's birth, the death of a *rakshasa* (monster), and prayers to make one healthy or wealthy. If the Indians were allowed to have long weekends and holidays for all these occasions, we would probably be left with 20 working days per year. Our home was not immune to any of these festivities, and we enjoyed them all.

The Navarathri celebration was an important nine days at our house. It was alive with flowers, decorations, and the sound of *Lalitha Sahasranamam,* a chant that is repeated for the nine days. Appa's flower vendor made sure that the rose petals, all wrapped in a banana leaf, would arrive at our place on time for the *poojai*. Appa loved flowers, and we all got a tutorial on flower-arranging at our home. We had every contraption you need to have the stems stand upright. He was the one who used to tell me to toss in aspirin. It was good for both the heart and the roses. The smell of roses brought our home alive, and the priest Suri Saastrigal would be at our place all of those nine days chanting the mantras or *slokhas* loudly for Appa to repeat after him.

The priest had long, flowing hair which would put the models for Pantene shampoo to shame. The front of his head was shaven in a half-moon shape. His curly hair was tied in a bun with a small flower tucked into it. His round bifocal eyeglasses had red frames, and the rim over the nose was held together by insulation tape where it had broken over the bridge of the nose. His garb was simple. Like most Indian men, he wore his *veshti* in *panchagachcham* style. Among the southern Indians, the *veshti* is worn as a wrap by married and unmarried men, but the *panchgachcham* style (where the material passes between the legs) was reserved for married men. Suri Saastrigal had on an *angavastram,* and his *poonal* (sacred thread) had a talisman hanging at the end. He had prayer beads around his neck, and we knew he commanded a lot of respect from our parents and elders.

"Children, you have to keep silent and observe the *poojai*."

"Okay."

As children, my sisters, friends, and I were more amused than awed by Suri Saastrigal's appearance. We were fearless, even though he would tell us to silently observe all the rituals he was performing with my father.

"Did you just see what happened?" I whispered to Prema.

"The flower from his hair has fallen on the floor," Prema replied giggling. "I think I'll put it on his hair."

"Go ahead," I egged her on.

Before long, she had stepped behind him to tuck the flower into the priest's bun. We all laughed together as Appa and Saastrigal turned around.

"What happened?"

"Oh, nothing," Prema replied impishly.

Amma took Prema into the kitchen. "Prema, any more mischief and you will be stopped from going out to play with your friends," she chided her.

"I got into trouble all because of you," Prema complained to me. Amma gave me her big-eyed stare and signed for me to behave or else I stood to be grounded too. Swathi, the "goody two-shoes," was sitting on Appa's lap, as she could do nothing wrong. Not for long. I was getting bored.

"Swathi, look behind you," I started it off with Swathi, as Prema was out of bounds. "You have something on your back," I said, tickling her back with a rose stem.

"Amma!" she let out a shriek and jumped off Appa's lap. I was satisfied that I had her off Appa's lap and quietly waited to decide on my next mischief. But that didn't happen, because Amma took the reins and I was told to clear the floor or behave.

All we were interested in was the *vadai* and *chakkraipongal* that my mother had done for *prasaadham* (offerings for God). I aped and mocked this priest, sitting behind him watching his bun unravel several times during the *poojai*. This is an important prayer offering to the Goddess Lalitha, the goddess of divine energy who is the combination of Lakshmi (Goddess of wealth), Saraswathi (Goddess of knowledge), and Parvathi (Goddess of strength).

By the way, the two important terms *Purusha* and *Prakriti* in Hinduism clearly talk about the two important states of humans on this earth and their interdependence. One cannot live without the other. This is the very essence of this prayer during Navarathri. Depending upon where you search for the meaning and what you read, it can be terribly confusing. Appa had books which convinced him that chanting was the road to serendipity, and he was able to conceptualize the very essence of the Upanishads and Vedas. When I asked him any question about these issues,

Relentless Brush Strokes

the explanations were long winded and confusing. If he could not be convincing, he could be terribly confusing to the simple-minded student.

At the end of it, I learned to appreciate the very interesting fact that in Hinduism *parmapurusha* governs this world. *Purusha* in literal translation, means "man." If you add a *parma* prefix, it becomes *parmapurusha,* which means "supreme being," or what we refer to as God. The best part is *Prakrit:* This all-too-powerful combination of strength, knowledge, and wealth is a woman who is necessary to create a supreme being from a man. So, *purusha* is a powerless creation of God without his counterpart, the *prakriti*? Well, Hinduism had laid out its beliefs and concepts with the utmost respect for women. There is no scripture in Hinduism that weakens a woman's status in this world. When, where, and why did some Hindu men fall out of the straight path and start to mistreat women? It is not written in scriptures.

When I took my six-year-old daughter to the local temple in Toronto, she saw the number of idols and deities that were placed in various parts of the temple. "Mom, did you not say that there was one God? Why is it that we Indians have so many Gods?" she asked.

I had to come up with a quick and smart answer otherwise, I stood to look like a dunce. Moreover, I was going to let down the traditional Hindu way of idol worship and all those billion followers, including myself, in the eyes of this impressionable child. I could only compare God to doctors. After all, I know doctors would like to think that they are God. "Well, kiddo, if you broke your leg, you would go to a bone specialist. If you had a heart problem, you would go to a cardiologist. In the same way, Hinduism is a highly specialized religion where you pray precisely to the correct God of your choice to fulfill your wishes." I had the right answer, I guess. She did not prod me, and I took her around the temple extremely happy with myself. Even Appa could not have come up with this brilliant comparison.

Not that I am a pro at Hindu spiritual teachings or a guru in the chanting of the prayers, but having lived with Appa and having heard some of these prayers chanted for the first twenty years of my life, I had learned some key teachings from Navarathri. This was the time for spiritual studies, and the nine days were spent celebrating in various ways all over India. The southern Indians offered their prayers to Parvathi, followed by Lakshmi, and then Saraswathi. The day after the Saraswathi poojai was Vijayadasami (victory on the tenth day), when we all read our books, played our music, or started any new ventures with the hope that we would be successful. When I was in ninth grade, Appa brought in a Carnatic music teacher on Vijayadasami to begin music lessons for my larynx. This poor music teacher may have faced many challenges, but he never in a million years thought he would be meeting the mother of all challenges. The tiny muscles in my throat could not let out two notes without their sounding like a croak. But to Appa's ears, whatever I sang sounded like music. He would patiently sit with me and practice even after the poor teacher fled from the city. I woke up one day and decided to put my imaginary hearing aids on. I realized that I had an ear for music, but not the larynx for it. That is when I switched to playing the guitar, and did I ever keep my poor Appa up with all the noise. He would patiently hear me practice in my room all afternoon. He and I would nod off to a restless sleep between my strumming and repeated errors.

"Moham," Appa said, "she keeps the whole neighborhood up when they want to have an afternoon siesta. And then when we are all up and about, your daughter is sleeping like a baby hugging her guitar."

"She will be going soon for her lessons, and then God alone knows if she is going to keep us up tonight," murmured Amma. It was not hard to get Appa interested in my guitar activities. Soon he would get his harmonium out and the two of us would create a racket together, much to my mother's chagrin.

The other festival in which Appa was our hero was Diwali, the festival of lights. Our favorite pastime was preparing for Diwali with him. It is the Hindu Christmas, if one really wanted to compare religions. Jesus was born on Christmas day, but for Hindus, Rama returned from fourteen years of exile to rule his kingdom. There is a lot of fanfare, and the highlights of this celebration are new clothes and playing with firecrackers. Appa was the biggest kid in the neighborhood, and he did not take this time of celebration lightly. We probably had the largest supply of firecrackers, which left all our friends to envy. Moreover, he was the first to wake up the entire neighborhood with the noisy red firecrackers he set off at 4 a.m. All my friends in the neighborhood would be up at 4 and he would be out with us all, "burning a lot of money to ashes," as my mother always said about this day. She liked only the sparklers, and we were into the bigger and better colorful noisy rockets and so on. The next best thing was the great time we all had, with the exchange of sweets and savories while we visited friends and family on Diwali day.

Appa was the only one I knew who could transform from an ultra-religious chanting moksha-seeking man into an earthly pleasure-seeking mortal. Always influenced by what others might say about this transformation and how his family would be perceived by others, this metamorphosis of Appa was not taken lightly at our place. He, on the other hand, did not think twice. He would change from a chanting holy man with prayers and mantras on his lips to sipping scotch on the rocks. For a moment, close your eyes and imagine Appa with his veshti around his waist, poonal across his torso, vibhuthi stripes adorning his body and his forehead, and a glass of Johnnie Walker whisky in his hand raised in cheers. Mahatma Gandhi said: "I think I have understood Hinduism correctly when I say that it is eternal, all-embracing, and flexible enough to suit all situations." This quote describes my God-fearing, Hindu-embracing, and flexible Appa.

Why could we not accept this model for a monk? Appa had transcended various planes with his invocation of God by his prayers and actions. Surely Johnnie Walker whisky and scotch are allowed means of transportation for salvation. We did not take this lightly and shunned this action of his. This was like being Jekyll and Hyde, my mother would say, and we all backed her.

"Why can't you be normal?" Amma rebuked him for his actions, especially if it involved any alcohol.

"You can drink once in a while. Forget it, yaar."

"It's okay for you to do this on an ordinary day, but why on a day when you have finished saying all your prayers?"

"I say my prayers everyday. According to you I should not drink anyday. I'm socializing with my friends and your brothers."

"Moham, we're there, don't worry," Paddu, my uncle, would come to Appa's rescue. My uncle was the scotch titration specialist. He played an even field between his sister and Appa. He kept the two of them happy while he enjoyed his drink with Appa.

"Let the music begin," Appa, now on some scotch, happily called, asking for the family to get out the guitar and harmonium and for all the ladies, men, boys, and girls to join in the living room and start the celebration while we enjoyed our dinner and dessert.

The day had just begun, and music would accompany traditional card games and Monopoly. Diwali—why is it that we cannot have this every month? I want to enjoy more with Appa, who is all loosey-goosey, and so are all the friends and family. Amma's fear was that Appa's spiritual inspirational state might become the norm for him. She would keep a leash on his habits, sometimes with success; and at other times his habits rode him to hurt him mortally.

"Moham, I must have had one too many," Appa confessed the next day. "I need ginger juice and strong coffee to shake this monstrous headache and heartburn."

Amma was not sympathetic and pointed out that he had no willpower and that all his prayers had not taught him self-control and serenity. Appa never understood Amma's principles, and vice-versa. He was convinced that his colorful portrait of the "art of living" was an appropriate combination of colors—pure hues and mixed variants that raised one from mere existence to salvation. What had serenity to do with scotch? His canvas for festivals consisted of splashes of bright and vivid colors, with various shades and values altered by his moods. The texture and manner with which his dexterous fingers were layering the imaginary paints decided the mood for the day. His family and friends could swing his strokes and actions from manic to melancholy on this pretend canvas. We played our cards well, and as usual Appa brought a successful end to a beautiful and memorable Diwali day.

Pongal is another important festival in the Hindu calendar. It happens in January and marks the beginning of the harvest. It may be the Indian Thanksgiving. The winter harvest has produced an abundance of rice from the paddy fields, and it is time to celebrate and thank the sun God. This celebration lasts for three days.

At Thatha's place, the last day was a big event, when the cows were honored for giving milk and the farm animals for a fruitful harvest. Who better to celebrate this event than Patti? She was at her best. All the cows were decorated and taken around the neighborhood by Gopal. Sweets and delicacies were exchanged, and they even rated whose cow looked the prettiest. Patti proudly displayed her beautiful cows. Whenever Appa was there with her, she had a great time with him. One time, Raji, her pet cow, somehow managed to take off on its own in its splendor, and Patti was hysterical. Her son became an instant hero when he found her standing around Lala's sweets store near the temple, busy chewing on banana leaves. He brought her home, and both Appa and Raji received a hero's welcome.

Appa was visiting me in Toronto when Patti was extremely sick. Poor Appa! He just did not know how to take a situation like this. Thatha's reaction was one of dejection. He had to show his displeasure on someone. Who better than Appa? He promptly wrote a letter to Appa and told him in no uncertain words that Patti was on her deathbed and that his absence had not made the situation any better. If her funeral were to take place, then they would not wait for him to return. Appa was mortified by the situation, and we consoled him that she would make it. He would see his mother. His love for his mother knew no bounds, and being deeply religious, his communication with the Almighty had now reached different heights. Patti's plans were different. She made it clear to the family that her cremation would not take place without her Ambi. Appa's brother and Thatha were not going to do something that she would not like. Patti passed away on Pongal day, when the cows were decorated for the parade. Her cows stayed at home out of respect to her. Appa reached Madras after Patti passed away, to perform his duties as the oldest son. Thatha was a broken man after having lived with Patti for sixty-five years. He could not be consoled.

Patti's demise was a turning point in Appa and Thatha's relationship. Patti may not have seen her husband's attitude soften toward their son, but the rest of us saw a different take on this new family movie directed by Thatha. Appa had a minor heart attack and Thatha heard of it. Thatha was a concerned and compassionate father toward his ailing son. "Ambi, I have seen all kinds of sorrows in my life," Thatha told him. "I do not want anything happening to you. Please take care of your health. Do all that is necessary to restore yourself to normal."

"Moham, my father is a changed man."

"He loves you. 'Blood is thicker than water,' " said Amma. Appa gloated as he basked in his father's love. Their renewed relationship brought a close to all differences they might have had in the past. For the first time, Appa and Thatha were enjoying each other's company, and I couldn't believe my eyes when I saw the two together. If we'd said that they had any problems between them, it would have made liars out of us.

CHAPTER 17
Clairvoyance

> (In Sanskrit)
> Om bhur bhuvah suvah
> Tat savitur vareniyam
> Bhargo devasya dhimahi
> Dhiyo yo nah prachidayat
>
> Oh God Thou art the giver of life,
> The remover of pain and sorrow,
> The bestower of happiness; creator of the
> Universe, may we receive Thy supreme,
> knowledgeable light;
> May thou guide and inspire our intellect in
> the right direction.
> —Gayatri mantra for soul freedom

Spiritualism and chanting of prayers, as I have mentioned, were exhibited mostly by Appa in the Swamy household. Interspersed in the daily activities were discourses on superstitions and religion with learned men, who would from time to time drop in to say hello to Appa. He was well respected for his knowledge of the Vedas and Upanishads.

When I was growing up, I never questioned Appa as to why I should believe in these activities. He did not expect us to follow him in his religious pursuits, and we did not see any reason for him not to accent his colorful personality with a sprinkle of the ancient teachings.

"Appa, do you really believe in what you are doing?"

"Yes. You have to believe in yourself."

"Appa, at school they tell me that if I don't pray to Jesus Christ, I won't go to heaven."

"At home you pray to Ishwaran, and at school you pray to Jesus," Appa taught. "Now you have the front seat in heaven! The Christians have named Ishawaran as Jesus. Jesus is just one of the reincarnations of the Hindu God. Don't stop praying to him."

So, I would continue with the prayers that I had been taught at school: "Our Father, who art in heaven, hallowed be thy name . . . " Not once had I stopped to question this belief. I continued with this simple prayer in front of our religious idols, as it was a mouthful to pronounce any of the Sanskrit words. On Sundays, I even attended Sunday school with my friends. Appa and Amma had no problem with that, as it was their solution for some healthy Sunday entertainment for their children. Between Father Rajan and some of Appa's Christian friends, we had some healthy comparative-religion discourses at home. If Buddha reincarnated to initiate Buddhism and Jesus reincarnated and Christianity was born, then it was okay for the Swamy clan to foster our belief in reincarnation.

Now, if you are skeptical about reincarnation or other metaphysical beliefs, then you might as well say that you are not a practicing Hindu. But Hindus are not the only mortals that believe there is life after death. When I was in Egypt, the Egyptians took this hope a whole notch further. They buried all their worldly possessions in hopes of retrieving their loot to reuse it in another life. Hindus cremated their dead and expected their soul to be reborn in another form. Now if I had to choose, I would opt for the Egyptian style to bid farewell to this world. If you die in the Egyptian fashion, one thing is certain: There will be food, clothing, jewelry, and lotus perfume when you wake up. These worldly possessions are givens for Egyptian mortals.

What does a Hindu get while bidding his final farewell to mother earth? Nothing. He depends on his karma. A man with a good karma will return as a good person to walk this world again (naked and hungry, I guess, as they did not plan as well as the Egyptians). If he had harmed others, he would get his share of punishments in the same lifetime or he would be reborn to be reprimanded. "Do unto others as they do unto you" or every action would have a serious consequence in your next life. If you did not reap the fruits of your bad deed, you were destined to be born again to receive the punishment owed you.

That was the basis of karma amongst Hindus. If you had killed too many ants or mosquitoes, then your soul might return as an ant or a mosquito. This philosophy and fear about the afterlife must have redirected a large sector of Hindus out of Hinduism into Jainism, where *ahimsa* (nonviolence) is the basis of the religion, and as a Jain they are set for their next life too. A Jain is expected to lead a life treating all animals with respect. Even though a Brahmin believes that he is the highest form, I for one do not know if there is any truth to this statement. If you asked a Sikh or a Jain, he may beg to differ too.

My father, a Brahmin, was a firm believer in reincarnation. The *Gayatri Japam* (mantra or prayer for the Gayatri), which teaches the mind divinity, and *Sandhyavandanam* worshipping before sunrise in the morning and before sunset were acknowledged actions from the days of the Vedas that he firmly deemed to be stepping stones to divinity. He was absolutely certain that this was his seventh and final birth. After all, he was a male Brahmin and his soul had finally reached the highest rung in the ladder of *moksha* salvation, toward becoming part of the *Brahman*, or Supreme Being. Because of my father's vast knowledge of metaphysics, Vedas, and Hinduism, he was a prey to the few who claimed to have parapsychological powers and extrasensory perception.

Relentless Brush Strokes

He met a man named Chandra at the local club who promised to assess my father's seven lives. Jackpot! Appa was the most excited man on the block. Our home had throngs of people coming to meet the clairvoyant, Chandra. All Chandra wanted was a free meal and a small fee to look into each person's past lives, and he would explain in detail as to why they had been born again into this world as men or women.

Chandra arrived at 10 a.m. and our home was buzzing with eager people waiting to hear about their past lives.

"I don't think you should fall for this," Moham chided. "He's trying to make a fast buck and you're a prime target. If you really believed that he was telling the truth, then let him continue. But there is no way to prove him to be correct."

"No, Moham," Appa insisted, "he is genuine and is definitely a clairvoyant. If he wanted to lie, he could have told us that he had been the king of England in one of his lives. But look at him. He was a reptile in one of his lives and he is happily sharing this story with us. I would be ashamed to relate this part of my reincarnation, but he is destiny- and duty-bound."

Chandra was being humble and realistic in his clairvoyance stories by subjecting himself in his past lives to being a reptile, a poor woman, etc. My mother was skeptical. "Somehow I can't understand the necessity to know anything about one's past life," Amma continued.

"How can you not believe him?" my father asked. "You have a too distrustful mind."

"Now, you just wait and see, for he is going to ask you questions about your present profession and interests, and based upon that he is going to weave a nice story that will please you," Amma said. She was not too far from the truth. "A lot of us have trouble handling this present life with care, let alone have a clairvoyant interject our present state with past phenomena," Amma continued to murmur with distrust.

Anyway, it began with the ringing of a bell. Chandra went into a trance. We all saw him close his eyes and call one by one the people who were interested in knowing their pasts. My father, the eager beaver, was absolutely ready and receptive to hear about his. He sat on the floor in the lotus position in front of Chandra, his eyes closed, detached from this world in an alpha mode of deep relaxation.

"Swamy, you have had six lives and this is your last life. You are a man with deep convictions who has done good karmas. Hence, you were always a human being and were never born as any other living thing. Your first life was in a temple in Karnataka, where you sculpted the temple and idols." Appa did not open his eyes to see the man who was communicating with him in this state of suspended animation, for fear that Chandra may lose his psychic communication powers. "In your second life, you were born as an artist in central India. You had met your present wife in one of your lives. You were a rich woman and she was your accountant. This is her payback life to you."

"Mom, I knew that something was not correct!" I whispered. "As an accountant, you must have pilfered some money from Appa in his past life. Look what you have to put up with in this present life because of your karma. You are so practical and now you'll be listening to what happened to you five lives ago. Well, this life should put you straight and hopefully you'll return as a Brahmin man to join the supreme being." I was visibly entertained by Chandra.

"Swamy, your daughter will be a doctor," predicted Chandra. "She will bring you the fruits of a karma yogi, as you do not have it in you to be a caregiver in this life."

Chandra was a smart man. He had noticed all the paintings, recognized my father's talents as an artist, and made up a story that would please Appa's palate. He had also noticed the *Gray's Anatomy* on the study table.

My maternal uncle had been arriving excitedly to hear about his own life when my father had blurted out to Chandra all the stories about my mother's family. Before you know it, this ESP sage found it easy to predict for my uncle based on his life's stories. Incidentally, Chandra also predicted our future for this life and I was curious to hear what he had to say for me.

Finally, Amma served lunch and *prasaadam* (offering to God) for all those who had gathered to hear Chandra. By the way, the *prasaadam* is not to be tasted by the cook before it is presented to God. This tests the culinary capabilities of any cook. Amma forgot to add the sugar into the *prasaadam*. Finally, after the *prasaadam* was blessed, it was given to all of us. But without sugar, it was not palatable.

"Moham, what happened? God has diabetes, I guess, as the *prasaadam* lacks the key ingredient."

The belief that nobody tastes anything before it is offered to God was very strong. For example, once when I was growing up, I was helping Amma prepare some *vadai*, fried lentil balls, and by mistake ate one before it was offered to God.

"Lalla, you are a big girl," Amma scolded me. "Surely, we do not eat the *prasaadam* before we offer it to God."

"I am sorry, Amma."

"Your daughter has tasted the *prasaadam*," Amma called out to Appa. "And now I have to make it all over again!" She was exasperated because it delayed the *poojai*, the religious chanting.

Appa was immediately at my side, supportive and consoling me. "Don't be so upset with her. After all, she is only eight years old." He immediately started to help

Relentless Brush Strokes

Amma so that she would not get further annoyed with me. He hated to see tears in his daughters' eyes.

As much as I think I am not very superstitious, it is hard to erase what has been embedded in my behavior patterns from childhood. I may not take off in alpha mode to seek salvation, but certain Hindu teachings that were practiced at my house are alive and well in me. One such practice is bowing in reverence before the elders with my hands held in front of me, called *namasthe*. *Namasthe* can be used to welcome or bid farewell to someone. It is a healthy way to greet anyone, and more of us should follow this healthy practice. It may help us to stop spreading infections and germs. The second level of *namasthe* is the *namaskaram*.

Namaskaram has a whole different meaning. We actually prostrate ourselves on the floor in front of the idol or whoever is older to us. Surya, the sun salutation (*namaskaram*), was practiced by Appa every day.

It was not uncommon for us to do the salutation or *namaskaram* if we wore a new sari to thank the Lord, followed by *namaskaram* to the person who gave it to us. This form of displaying our respect to elders was not taken lightly by the Swamy family.

Appa and Amma never had any problems doing this toward anyone who came to our place, especially if the men and women were between sixty and eighty years of age. He would even hold his ears and nose and say his prayers in front of the man out of respect. This annoyed us when we were young teenagers, as he expected us to do the same to anyone who came to our place. One time, an elderly couple came to visit us in hope of getting my sister to marry their grandson.

"Appa, please don't ask me to do *namaskaram* to them," my sister beseeched him. "Their grandson, or whoever, isn't even here, and they expect a sneak-peek preview of our family. And you may want us all to do *namaskaram*. You go ahead, but I will not!"

My *uncle Paddu* was visiting us when this couple arrived. Well, good luck! If *namaskaram* was the sole criterion to make or break this deal, then they were in for a surprise. My sister was not about to stoop for anyone. Her body language was screaming "No deal!" with every gyration. Appa and Amma saw that they were an elderly couple and that it would not be wrong to progress from *namasthe* to *namaskaram*. After all, we were Hindus, and the teachings were that we show our respect to all *athithis*, guests. And so they did the salutation.

"Mama and Mami, let me do *namaskaram* to you two," said Appa as soon as all the refreshments were served and everyone was comfortable. My sister glared at my parents and refused to budge from the chair.

"If you want to do this, I don't object," she hissed into my mother's ear. "But leave me alone."

"Mama and Mami, I am Moham's brother, and this is my wife," Paddu said. "We also want to take your blessings." He was a faithful follower of his sister and brother-in-law. He also looked eagerly toward my sister, hoping that she would have a change of heart and follow the elders of the family. Nothing would pry her away from her seat. She was pissed off with the family for even entertaining two boring old people, and what nerve to expect all to prostrate in front of strangers.

When the elderly couple left, Paddu said with tongue in cheek, "Moham, whenever you have an occasion and you need anyone to do *namaskaram,* you can count on me." He knew that my sister had been showing her displeasure about the whole ordeal.

I thought that I had shed this habit too, like my sister. Except for bowing in front of God, I extended *namaskaram* only to my parents. Then one day, I was at my friend's house, where I met a family visiting Toronto from Calcutta. As soon as they heard that I was Swamy's daughter, they came over to greet me warmly. "Hello, I knew your parents in Calcutta. We were very good friends, and your father was a well-known figure in the Ved Bhavan. We had a great time with him in Calcutta."

This was an elderly couple, about eighty years of age or above, who had known my father for over thirty years. These were new criteria, and I was slowly rising in my own mind to become the daughter that Appa would have liked to see. I have no idea what possessed me that day. "Please let me do *namaskaram* to you two," I said, and before you know it, I was on the floor in front of a large crowd doing my *namaskaram*—the age-old traditional way, taking my blessings from this elderly couple. Appa's spirit may have burrowed into that crowded room. He may have eagerly waited for his daughter to finally start showing respect the way Hindus are expected to do.

Well, what do you know? I have transformed. *Namaskaram* has been revived, Appa. It is alive and well. Look at what your daughter is doing. Toronto, Timbuktoo—hang loose Appa. You have taught well. Even my children practice this in front of the religious idols.

From the Swamy household, Appa's DNA in his children was slowly transcribing a picture on this new pretend canvas laid out in Canada. The traditions, teachings, and rituals are still alive, and immortalization of the Hindu culture continues in Swamy style 12,000 miles away on the North American continent.

CHAPTER 18
Classical Appa

I cannot remember the first day I heard Carnatic music. I probably heard it in my mother's womb. My father enjoyed music, especially classical music. When our parents had a get-together, music and great food were the two staples that brought our circle of friends closer to us. Some of my uncles, aunts, and cousins were amateur singers, and the gathering of our clan spelled an all-night display of talents. Even I, who professed to be no singer, would try my skill in the comforts of home.

Dad strongly believed in music and its healing powers. My mother got her share of music education from my father. Today, research has shown that there is a surge in the neurohormones, melatonin, norepinephrine, and epinephrine as we listen to music. My dad said that the healing powers of Indian classical music had long been known in India. When the ragas are skillfully played, sung, and listened to at certain hours of the day, you receive the appropriate therapy that it is supposed to render. We had an excess of neurohormones and melatonin levels during these parties. Let us not underestimate the whisky, scotch, and beer flowing through my dad's, uncles', and cousins' veins. The women did not indulge in any alcohol. I may have had a sip or two from my dad and uncles, but I did not understand the importance of imbibing alcohol for pleasure.

The very essence of Indian classical music is the *raga*, which is set in ascending and descending scales. The rendering of these ragas can be variegated by the stress put on the notes by a voice or instrument, with, of course, rhythm and time. These ragas are played at certain times of the day and certain seasons to have the finest effect on our audio apparatus, transporting the therapeutic waves to our ever-eager brains. I for one could not use this skill and practice on my sick patients. First of all, the right note may not hit the sick cells and I stood to never see my patients again. So I bid farewell to singing as a hobby at a very early age.

Some of the ragas that are played in the mornings are Bhairev, Bhairevi, Bhoopali, and Bilavel. The ragas that are created for evening and night pleasure are Kafi, Yamen, Malkauns, and Neelambhari.

Ragas alter a person's mood and depicts and invokes any one of the *nava rasas* (nine emotions) that human beings are slaves to. These emotions form the basic neural network of a human psyche. The *nava rasas* are:

- Adbhuta—curiosity, awe and wonder

- Bhibhathsa—hopelessness and vengefulness
- Bhayankar—fear
- Hasya—laughter and happiness
- Karuna—sorrow and pity
- Rudra—anger
- Veera—bravery and majesty
- Shantham—calmness, peace and contentment
- Shringara—love, beauty and passion.

There are countless compositions in various ragas, especially when devotional songs are being created. The difference is that Indian classical music has given a name to every mood that a certain raga can collate. Some of them have "crossed over" to film music, and I was surprised when I heard Indian music being played in some non-Indian restaurants in Toronto.

You can imagine our home when we had classical music sung and we debated as to what raga the song was set to and where it hit the right pitch to bring on the right emotional reaction. When we went to some of the concerts with my father, he would be highly critical if the artist was not up to the standard. One time, he said it quite aloud: "It is time that this musician retired and stuck to singing in the shower behind closed doors!" We were very embarrassed, as the musician's sister was seated next to us at the concert. My mother looked apologetically at her, and I moved to the next seat and tried to avoid father and pretended that I did not know him.

Father brought music to his paintings. I asked him to copy a Monet for me. "Monet, Van Gogh, or for that matter any artist or anybody is unique, and even God cannot create two identical people. This is dharma, or your exclusive signature," my dad responded to me philosophically. "I will try to do a painting by which you will see the sunrise like I see it. It may not be a Monet, but for you it will be your personal Monet from me. I will create a style where you will hear the morning raga. This will be my 'Impressionist sunrise' for you."

The painting, in vivid cadmium orange and chrome orange, depicted clouds and sunrays of all feisty colors. From his imaginative color wheels, he created the beautiful sun shining with cadmium and lemon mixed with glazes of titanium white. The waves in the ocean were rhythmically beating against the tree at the side. The sun was creating the music on the instrument, the ocean; and the mood was set to *adhi thaala* (eight-beat rhythms) in the raga Bhairavi. The painting brings on a serene, calm state of mind. I have started to meditate in front of this artwork, as it de-stresses me and prepares me for the day's work.

Appa could not leave this painting standing alone. "What do you say? Morning is followed by night. Let me paint the night raga for you," he said. He created the moonlight as the mirror image of the sunrise. The mood and rhythm in this painting was skillfully altered by Appa's fingers. His favorite colors, Prussian blue and ultramarine blue, have been lavishly spread amongst the cobalt and cerulean blue. The titanium white is smiling through all this in the form of the moon. "You can change the rhythm and listen to my favorite raga Malkauns in the moonlight," said my dad. "It reminds me of my trip down the Rhine river with your mother." He sat pensively in front of the painting whistling the Blue Danube waltz, a far cry from the raga Malkauns.

Appa said, "Now do you see, if I tried to imitate Monet or Van Gogh I would not have done a good job, but when I brought my personal strokes, the creation is different and at the same time it will not be discarded as a poor copy of a great artist. This is *swaya-dharma,* a teaching in Gita, our old scriptures. This world would be a better place if we did not try to look like the pretty and thin model or for that matter try to act like one of the movie stars. A monkey does not imitate a cat, nor a dog a bird. Their intelligence is far superior to ours. They are not trying to mimic one another." This was Appa's lesson for me to be myself.

In my eyes, his painting is of a non-starry, moonlit, beautiful night where I worship the moon and dejectedly think of what my dad had told me about himself: "I am a cross between Monet and Vincent Van Gogh in my moods," he'd said cheerfully.

His passion was painting buildings and temples. My favorite piece is the Tanjore temple to Lord Brahadeeswara. My sister-in-law had just returned from her trip to Tanjore. She brought back memorabilia of paintings, and Appa's attention was caught by the photograph that she had taken of this temple. She gave him this picture, and I don't think I saw Appa for a few days. He was bent over the canvas drawing the temple with precision and skill. This was not the first time I saw this temple immortalized by my father. His last few paintings of the temple were given away to acquaintances who visited our family. Appa was generous about giving away his paintings. He said he could always do another and that it was only a canvas and frame with paint thrown on it. "I do not have the walls to hang all the paintings I have created. It might as well hang in some home."

Appa's depiction of the temple pillars are like the pipes of a church organ. You can almost hear the music from the very core of these pillars, just like the musical *Mani Mandapam* in a temple in Tamil Nadu state. The Nandi has turned into stone listening to this never-ending music emanated from these pillars in this artwork. At the Tanjore temple, the pillars do not create music. An expressive delight brought about by Appa in all of his paintings.

One time, Appa was busy painting and I was busy playing my guitar. Amma had to run errands and left the kitchen in our hands. Big mistake!

"The pressure cooker is on and it will make two loud whistles," Amma instructed me as she closed the door behind her. "Do not forget to turn off the stove after the second whistle."

"I will turn it off, don't worry," I said.

The pressure cooker must have whistled, hissed, and quaked. Nobody budged. It called out again and again and we did not hear. It must have done everything that a pressure cooker could do to get attention. The two artists were too engrossed in their rooms. Then came a loud bang from the kitchen. Appa and I ran together toward it.

"What is it?"

"I don't know Appa."

"Oh, my God! Look what has happened here!" Appa stood in the middle of cooked rice, lentil, and potatoes that had been hurled in all directions. The pressure cooker had literally blown its top. A colorful mess of all three staples was smeared on the floor, roof, and walls.

"Appa, I forgot all about it," I confessed. "Now, I'm going to be in big trouble when Amma walks in. What am I going to do?"

"Well, we have a lot of work to do. Let's start with the ceiling." So Appa was arched over standing on a table clearing the mess created on the ceiling due to my absent-mindedness.

"Appa, you look like Michelangelo painting the ceiling of the church in Rome," I jokingly compared him to one of his favorite artists.

"Well, he left something for the world to see. But I, after clearing this stucco of rice and lentils, will have to repaint the ceiling, but before that we better have some rice and lentils ready for Mom." Appa consoled me, "This will be our secret." He got the kitchen to look normal again and I helped him get the pressure cooker ready. This time we sat in the kitchen to avoid any more mishaps, listening to every noise the pressure cooker made.

When Amma walked in, she was surprised that the cooker was still too hot to open. She had two eager helpers ready to assist her in the kitchen. We did not want her to notice anything that may have gone amiss.

CHAPTER 19
At the Movies with Appa

"We are going to the movies and Appa is taking us out for dinner," announced my mother excitedly, as we returned from school one Friday afternoon. We dressed up, and Mom took us by streetcar to the Metro Cinema. This was located on a major street corner in Calcutta, and was famous for showing only English movies. Appa would be meeting us outside the theatre. We were excited about the unexpected, exciting evening that Appa had planned for us.

"Mom, will you buy us chips and popcorn?" I pestered her. "I can't wait to see inside this theatre. I don't remember ever being to a movie here." I went on and on about the upcoming evening.

"Prema, please hold on to Lalla's hand," Mom said. "I do not want you getting lost. I will take care of Swathi."

The tram trip was very interesting. It went through some crowded marketplaces and then passed a wide scenic avenue built by the British. We thoroughly enjoyed the ride but were impatient to meet up with Appa. His workplace was just a stone's throw from the

Metro Cinema, and it should not have taken him long to pop down to the theatre to see his eagerly awaiting family. The movie was to start at 5:30 p.m., and we were there by 5. For half an hour we watched the crowd queue up to enter the theatre.

"Amma, the movie will start and I don't see Appa anywhere," I said to my mom.

"He should be here soon," Amma replied anxiously. I could see that she was a little worried too, as she had three eager children waiting to see the movie and she did not want them to be disappointed.

"It's 6 o'clock and Appa hasn't shown up," she finally said. "Something must be wrong. I'm sorry, girls. Let's go back. We'll catch the movie another day. First of all, we have to find Appa." My mother tried to console three really downcast and disheartened children. "You don't want to be sitting in a movie hall if Appa isn't well, do you?"

We three nodded our heads and accepted the turn of events, and we all returned home. (No cell phones in those days!) Prema was dragging her feet and I was picking on her to get her to act out so that Mom would give her a piece of her mind for not behaving herself. I wanted to do something and I was irritating and teasing my sisters and being a brat to catch my mother's attention.

Before long, we arrived home. Amma was shocked to see the front door wide open. "I'm sure I locked it before we left for the movie. Oh, my God! I hope it's not a robbery." She treaded in through the open door carefully, fearing that some thief might jump out at her. What do you know? Appa was relaxing; sitting on the easy chair munching peanuts and reading a book, oblivious to everything.

"Where did you all go?" Appa welcomed us cheerfully with open arms. "I came early, as I wanted to spend the time with you all."

"Where do you think we were?" My mother glared at him accusingly. Amma is the most beautiful woman I know. Her sweet nature cannot be paralleled, but Appa had turned her knobs the wrong way. She can spew out anger through her eyes, which we have all been on the receiving end of at one time or another. That day, Appa was the target. He apologized for having forgotten his date with the family and promised to make up for it in some other way. Appa knew how to make up for his errors, and we were happy to be at the receiving end of his generosity. He treated us all the next day, and he and Amma made up too, as Amma was making coffee and Appa was happily chatting away with friends who had dropped in to hear the story.

There are many movie stories we paint around Appa, and the memorable ones I can remember go back to the time when he took us to see *The Sound of Music*. He sang "you are sixteen going on seventeen" all the way to the restaurant after the movie. It was my sixteenth birthday, and he was the happiest man in town, announcing it to the world, as I embarrassedly thanked strangers who wished many happy returns. The long and short of it was that we all turned out to be movie buffs like our Appa. One thing we had learned in the process was to not trust Appa to buy the tickets. But our forgetful father, a faithful fan of movies, was ever eager to accompany us to an English film.

"Hey, Appa, this week is Audrey Hepburn week at the Globe Theatre," I said eagerly. "Are you interested in catching some of her good old movies? I think *Roman Holiday* is on as a matinee. I'm thinking of getting some tickets for some of her movies."

There was an advantage to going to the movies with parents when you were a teenager. You did not have to spend your own pocket money. Moreover, Appa would drive me there. I did not have to go in a crowded bus, which was what would happen if I went with my friends. You would never catch Appa on a bus. So, I picked up the tickets as I was returning from school.

"I picked up the tickets for *Roman Holiday* and *My Fair Lady*," I announced excitedly.

"Oops! You didn't tell me about picking tickets for *My Fair Lady*," Appa said apologetically. "I saw that movie today when you were at school."

"Appa you can't be trusted when Audrey is in town," I replied smilingly. "Never mind. I'll take a friend for the movie."

Appa loved Lucille Ball and Audrey Hepburn. He loved watching *I Love Lucy* on TV, and it was heartbreaking to see Appa mourn Audrey Hepburn's death when he himself was quite ill. Audrey too had suffered from cancer, and we did not have the heart to discuss her state with him when he was slowly losing physical strength, even though his will to live was strong.

He did not enjoy Bollywood movies and did not think much of people who watched them. Even as an opinionated fan of English movies, he would never pass a chance to accompany us to any movie, as he loved to come with us. But I am not sure if we loved his company in the movie theatre.

"Appa, this is our favorite Rajesh Khanna at his best," my sister Prema informed him as a matter of fact. "I don't want to be disturbed by any of your sighs or derogatory comments about him. So, if you are prepared to sit back and enjoy it, then you're on." (By the way, she was very serious about this hot movie star, and for that matter we all drooled over him.)

Prema was going with Appa to the movie, but she had forgotten the tickets at home. The two of them drove each other up the wall as she searched for the tickets in her huge handbag with many compartments.

"Prema, did you plan to bring your movie star back in your sack? Why couldn't you bring a smaller bag for the movies?" remarked Appa when he saw her extra-large bag, which may have served the purpose.

"Appa, you are not being a big help. I didn't ask you to come with me. It must be somewhere in my bag. Just help me look for it." She was annoyed with him and gave him an "if looks could kill" gaze. Something clicked. "I think I know where it is," she said. "I changed my purse and it's in the other purse, Appa. Well, let's go back home."

The two of them hurried home, and we stared at them as they walked in. The tension between Prema and Appa had grown pretty taut, and Appa was not even sure he wanted to go with her anymore.

"Moham, she may have lost the ticket," Appa explained, expecting support and sympathy from his wife. "But she remembered having changed her handbag. Is it my fault that she changed her handbag and left the ticket in the wrong bag? I raced behind her as fast as I could. I almost thought I was going to lose her in the crowd. My heart was beating so fast that I could hear it thumping in my ears. When I sat next to her, she gave me a look as if I was the reason behind today's mishap."

"Don't worry," my mother said. "She's going through her other purse, and I'm sure she'll find it. You may miss a few trailers and commercials, but who cares about those?"

Finally, Prema found the tickets and the two were ready to leave for the movies. Appa looked earnestly at my mother and said that she had better give him some Gelusil tablets, as he was feeling some tension and heartburn from running back and forth in this hot, humid weather. "I can imagine doing this for a good English movie," he declared. "What a father has to do for his daughter!" He raised his arms toward the sky in a helpless gesture as he departed with Prema.

Prema and Appa reached the theatre on time. The movie had just started, and they had great seats, as in India all movie seats are reserved and she had picked good tickets. Appa sat relaxed in his seat for ten minutes. The movie was the usual love story. Rajesh Khanna was a poor man had fallen for a girl from a wealthy family. The catchy tunes that the hero was lip-synching made him look groovy and handsome, and my sister was not about to blink or for that matter glance over to see why my father was squirming helplessly by her side. The hot scenes started to roll in, and Prema was savoring the fact that there was nobody better looking than Rajesh.

"Prema, I have this tight feeling in my chest. My pulse is racing and I'm not feeling good. I might be having a heart attack," Appa said, hoping that she would abandon this poorly made movie and go home. When Appa did not like something, he feigned angina. He may have suffered from heartburn, but not a heart attack. Appa's expressionism had reached a climax. He was bent over gripping his uneasy, squeamish stomach in a pose that could be difficult to achieve when you were sitting in a tight space. But Appa was a pro at all forms of yoga and confidently displayed his pain on a newly prepared canvas. Picasso's depictions in his blue period and Munch's Expressionistic paintings of *The Scream* and *A Sick Child* would take second to the art created by Appa's imaginative brushstrokes of '*My State of Mind* ' to my sister Prema that day.

"Appa, just have your Gelusil," Prema angrily retorted. "Mom just gave you a handful. You know you're okay. You just don't want to see the movie and you're cooking up an excuse." You may have seen fans in your time, but Prema was a hard-core, diehard fan of Rajesh. She was not about to walk away from this movie when it has just started.

"Prema, which one of us is more important to you: Rajesh or your *Appa,* who may die from a heart attack? I can feel the heat rush up to my head."

"Appa, you always do this. When you don't care for something, you want to get out of that place. I know you. So please sit down. Just a few more hours and we can go home." Prema tried to console him. But Appa continued to gyrate, writhe, and fidget in his seat from his heartburn. This was attracting attention from others in the audience, who gave Prema stares, and some even asked her to take her *Appa* to the emergency clinic, as he was looking pale beneath all those layers of Indian sun-kissed tan, which was even obvious in the darkened cinema hall.

"These are not like English movies, short and sweet," Appa said. "They have just started singing and chasing each other around trees. He has still not caught her. I do not see the end coming. Please let us go. This is not going to improve your knowledge, nor is Rajesh going to leave this girl to come home with you," implored Appa.

"Who is talking about marrying Rajesh Khanna or his look-alike?" Prema hissed. "Moreover, it is a Hindi movie, not a documentary. I am not at school, and I don't need to be educated. Please, Appa, keep quite." Prema was quite exasperated with Appa's indigestion drama.

She was not very successful. Appa had no sympathy for the lovesick impoverished lothario portrayed by Rajesh Khanna in a not very riveting performance, and his manipulative lover irritated Appa more than indigestion and heartburn. Appa's patience was dwindling. And what do you know?—he won. His expressionistic painting deserved an "A." After all, Appa was none other than the son of a movie director. He and Prema returned home at once, and Prema was not about to speak to Appa for terminating her movie prematurely.

My mother saw the two come through the front door. Prema's body language spoke about the past few hours. "What's the matter, Prema? The two of you are back so soon? Is everything alright with you two? You don't look good."

Prema was so annoyed with Appa that she refused to answer. As soon as Appa came home, his indigestion, heartburn, and "might be" heart attack all subsided to just a few hunger pangs. Mother's crispy *dosa* with sambhar and chutney cured his gastric reflux, and he went about painting a landscape. Appa was happy to portray bright and beautiful scenery on this canvas.

When Appa was visiting me in Toronto, Swathi and I asked him if he wanted to come to a movie. He was as ever ready as usual. We reminded him of Prema's trip with him to the Rajesh movie. He wore a big mischievous grin. When we went to the theatre, I asked Appa if he wanted popcorn or ice cream. He said both and Coke. We bought a large bucket of popcorn. He disappeared into the theatre with the bucket in his hand.

"Swathi, where's Appa? I thought he was going to sit with us and share the bucket of popcorn."

We saw him when the movie ended. He'd sat by himself to watch the show.

"Appa, how come you abandoned us? We wanted to sit next to you and have fun as you shared the popcorn."

"You both will constantly chat and disturb me in a good English movie," Appa replied sagely. "I will sit next to you for a Hindi movie, where you do not have to see or understand. They break into a song every five minutes and you can make up your own story from the songs."

CHAPTER 20
Appa Meets His Son

It was December 20, and Appa was quite vehement that he was not moving out of Calcutta. "The month of December is not auspicious, and I am not allowing my daughter to get married. This man has waited all these years; he can surely wait another month for the arrival of the auspicious month of Thai. Then and only then will I allow this marriage to happen."

"Appa, I am going to marry him," I said stubbornly. "But I will not do this without your blessings. You have to come to Mumbai as soon as possible."

"I am not going to move from Calcutta."

"Please, Appa, understand the dilemma you're putting me through."

"All I want you to do is postpone for a month."

"You haven't even met him. Please come," I begged Appa.

"No."

I had one ace card which I did not want to use on Appa. He would resent me if I called Thatha for his help.

But I was hanging by a string, and Amma could not convince Appa. So I finally drew the last card.

"Thatha, I want to get married, and Appa wants me to postpone it, as December is not an auspicious month."

"I just don't understand your *Appa*. All those religious activities have not given him any insight into a young girl. Let me speak to him."

Appa was on his way to meet his future son-in-law. My sister was accompanying him, and lord alone knows how much he fussed about this issue with her. I met the two of them at the station.

"You're lucky that both of us have arrived safely," my sister said. "Appa troubled me so much that only one of us was going to attend your wedding and it was going to be me." That evening he went to meet my future husband and in-laws.

"You are marrying a great man," Appa told me, and I knew that when he made a statement like that, he had not paid any attention.

"What was it that you liked about him?"

"They had a beautiful piano and a beautiful painting from Hong Kong hung above the piano," he answered, ignoring my question.

"Appa, you were focused on the painting, weren't you?"

"Maybe, but I couldn't help it, as the painting was beautiful."

"Appa, did you at least say hello to him and make some conversation?"

"I think I did. But all I can remember now is the beautiful painting."

"Appa, you are exasperating."

"Forget it, *yaar*. You'll be okay. His family seems nice."

Appa had a great time at the wedding, and I knew in my mind that he was going to miss me when I left India for Canada.

"Guess what I've planned. I'm going to paint the same colors for you in a sunset scene. The one I saw at your in-laws' place." Appa was still in the world in which he'd set eyes on the beautiful painting above the piano at my in-laws' house.

My heart was heavy as I bid farewell to my family. What I carried all the way with me on the flight was my dowry—the painting of the sunset scene that Appa had created after having met my husband. I was off to see the sunrise in Toronto.

My husband and he had a great rapport. My dad found a son in him, and they would spend hours together fixing a shed, gardening, pruning trees, or simply going to the Beaver lumberyard for some four by fours. My dad took on a more supervisory role and would direct my husband to do things around the home. One day after a tornado had split a tree into half, my dad and my husband went to the tree doctor and got some advice about how to protect the tree stump from rotting.

I was taking a nap and I heard a chain saw, and lo and behold my husband was on top of this 50-foot tree with the chain saw and my father was at the bottom holding on to a ladder. I came running down the stairs to stop this madness. "Who on earth would dream of sending his son-in-law up this high tree with a chain saw?" I asked disapprovingly. "That's a sure recipe for a widow maker."

My mother and I were upset at the two men. They walked in sheepishly after an unsuccessful attempt at trimming the broken stump of the large evergreen tree. Many of these episodes that frequently happened at our place were toasted with a glass of beer after my dad would remind my husband, "Shanks, you must be thirsty!"

One time my dad and mom were babysitting their two grandchildren when we were away for two weeks. My dad, who enjoys his glass of beer, was treated to a 24-pack by my husband. When we returned from our holiday, we noticed that my dad had not touched the beer.

My father mischievously looked at me and said, "Oh, I was too busy helping your mom with the children. Who has the time to drink?" I somehow could not believe that my dad could have gone dry for two weeks, especially when the beer was just a few feet away. Two weeks later I met my friend at the clinic and she said that she had gone to visit my parents. Her husband, Vic, had treated my dad to a pack of beer. The mystery was solved. My dad wore a sheepish grin when I confronted him about my friend's visit.

One time we were driving through Pennsylvania to visit a temple in Monroeville. In the seventies there was one Hindu temple in all of North America, and the Indians flocked to it. We wanted Amma and Appa to see this marvel. The fall colors were breathtaking and beautiful. When one lives in the tropics, change of colors is not something we see. We stopped at least fifteen times to get out of the car for Appa to take in the beauty and paint the colors on his pad. Appa could not hold his excitement, as fall colors were something that he had seen only in pictures. We all lived the excitement through his eyes. Even though I had seen the colors before, it brought a new meaning to me. As soon as we returned home, Dad was lost for two months creating a 5-foot canvas of fall colors. His son-in-law catered to all his whims and fancies. Appa was impatient and could not wait to stretch his own canvas. He breathed, ate, and slept near his painting.

The relationship that Appa and my husband had was very special. They enjoyed each other's company and became great friends. When Appa had to return to India after visiting us in Toronto, he said, "It's like visiting my son's home. I just had to watch out with my daughter, who has turned into a daughter-in-law."

CHAPTER 21
End of Thatha's Era

"Swathi, I had a weird dream last night. Thatha has been sick and I've been thinking of him a lot. I dreamt that he came up to me and blessed me. Now, I think he might have died." I sadly related my dream to my sister. Well, I was not too far off. My mother called me to say that Thatha had passed away peacefully.

"Don't dream about *me*," said my sister. "It must be some ESP, to dream about him and he dies the same day."

Appa and Amma were by his side. Over the years, Thatha had mellowed. He became close to his sons and daughters.

"Ambi, I want you to say the *Gayatri* mantra in my ears, as you are my oldest son," Thatha said to Appa. Thatha was spiritual but not overtly religious. As he told me once, "I may not be a regular visitor to the temple, but I do believe in saying my prayers privately." I have accompanied him many times around the garden collecting flowers for his morning prayers.

When Thatha's ability to comprehend and clear thinking prevailed, he proudly looked at his sixty-year-old son and said "Ambi, I am so proud of your accomplishments. You have a great wife who sailed with you and steered you toward a normal life. Look at you, a proud grandfather to four grandchildren. Your children love you. They respect you and are not fearful of you." This was a confession by a truly great man. No man wants to accept that he should have done different as a father.

"Moham, in my next life I would like to see you as Ambi's mother. You might bring out the best in him, and he may even fulfill his dreams of being an artist. I failed to let him do what he is best at," Thatha confessed as he reflected on his life sadly.

Bingo! I better go and search for that clairvoyant who ended Appa's seven sacred lives and said that this life was the grand finale. Chandra, you are wrong! Thatha's wishes may come true, and Appa, you may be back for another seven lives' cycle on mother earth. Cats have nine lives and we Hindus have seven. You better prepare your canvas. The scenery and the people may change their roles. I am just deciding my role in Appa's life. Do I want to be Appa's father, sister, brother, or wife? Or does Thatha want to return as Amma's husband? Good luck, Mom. If Thatha is to return as Amma's spouse, then I better chose one of the other roles. Or better still, I should call up that clairvoyant and ask him for the best role for the awesome roller-coaster ride that I can prepare for in my next life with Appa.

Thatha was the pillar of support, and Appa broke down and cried when the end came. Whatever differences of opinion the two had, all was ironed out toward the end. When I met Thatha two months before he passed away, he was happily interacting with his two sons, grandchildren, and great-grandchildren. There were no differences of opinion. There was no tension, and Appa had painted a portrait of Thatha. He proudly showed this to me.

"I wish I had spent more time with my children instead of pursuing a career that took a large part of my life out of my home," Thatha told me. My mellowed *thatha* really wanted to spend time with my father. I was trying to imagine what might have happened if Thatha had been there for Appa. Appa might have made a living as an artist. With Thatha's business skills, he may have even been successful.

CHAPTER 22
The Fatal Fracture

> It doesn't matter who my father was; it matters who I remember he was.
> —Anne Sexton

About 11 a.m. on a Friday, Amma called me at work. "Amma, you sound so upset."

"Appa went to see the dentist here in Los Angelas, who said that his tooth pain was from a loose tooth and he pulled the tooth out," Amma explained.

"Well, that's good. He'll be okay."

"Now Appa is in excruciating pain and he is not able to even take his hands from his jaw."

"Did the dentist do an X-ray before he took the tooth out?"

"Yes, he did. He told Appa that there was a cyst under the tooth, and that may be the reason why his tooth was loose." I was a little nervous about the cyst. What if the dentist had mistaken a cancer for a cyst?

"Amma, please ask Swathi to take him to the ER. This may be more than we know."

"She has just taken him there. That's why I am calling you, as I am worried."

"Please don't be worried. It's not going to help. Ask Swathi to call me when she returns from the ER."

Appa was not well and he was in excruciating pain. This now worried me. My sister returned with Appa from the ER and called me immediately. He had a fracture of the mandible, and they had referred him to a maxillo-facial surgeon. He was heavily sedated to control the pain.

I knew in my heart that this was not good news. But I waited to hear what his surgeon was going to do about the fracture. All I was praying for was that Appa had a benign cyst with a fracture through the mandible.

I had a hospital Christmas party. Appa enjoyed Christmastime. I was dressed to go even though I had an empty feeling inside. "Just mingling with others will take your mind off Appa," my husband said. "Moreover, you are 3000 miles away. What can you do about it?"

The phone rang and I did not want to pick it up. It was a collect call from the surgeon in LA. He gave me the bad news about the cancer in his jawbone. He said that this needed immediate care, as he had a fracture through the cancerous tumor. For me as a doctor, the level of terror set in faster than in a layperson. At that moment the fear of the disease and what it was going to subject my father to was crippling my senses. I could not move. My world was crumbling under me. What were we going to do with Appa? I did not go anywhere. I just sat down and helplessly went through in my mind what the immediate issues were that we needed to deal with. I called my friends, and they were all willing to do the surgery in Toronto.

"Amma, you can bring Appa to Toronto and we can have him undergo his surgery here," I told Amma. She was so heartbroken with the news that she broke down and wept.

Within a day Appa had made a decision. He wanted to return to India. "I have friends and family and I do not want to be here where I would be burden to my daughter, who is busy with her work. In India I have my sisters, brother, and friends." I respected Appa's feelings. India has good surgeons too. I knew he would be in good hands.

"Amma, I am so angry with the dentist. Appa should sue him for having been so careless. He should have been more careful and consulted the X-ray with an expert before taking out the tooth. This would have avoided the fracture," I said.

"Well, your Appa is different. He has painted a large painting for his dentist. Appa feels that if the dentist had not fractured his jaw, the diagnosis of cancer may have eluded him for a longer time. This is his way of thanking him for making the diagnosis."

"Amma, Appa should give him a piece of his mind not a piece of art. Tell the dentist that I am going to sue him for pain and suffering." I wept as I helplessly vented the anger that was building in me.

"No, Lalla. I didn't send you to medical school to have such anger toward another doctor. He did his best for your father. Your *Appa* thinks that this dentist was destined to diagnose his cancer, which is his karma. He deserves a painting from him. He also feels that we can't evaluate the doctor's capability by one mistake. So, your Appa will never take that course of suing anybody."

The arrangements were made with the help of my brother-in-law Vasan and his wife, Hema. Appa flew from Los Angeles straight to Mumbai. Vasan and Hema took Appa to the Tata Cancer Hospital, where he received his treatment for the next two years. He spent a lot of time with Vasan and Hema. Hema was Appa's love. He even started to treat her like his very own daughter. They had a very special relationship. Vasan and all my brothers-in-law would take turns visiting my parents during these sobering days.

My only fear was that Appa was going to be in a lot of pain. I was so wrong. This strong man had conquered his disfiguring cancer. He continued to do what he enjoyed most. He spent a lot of his time with my sister Prema. He waited eagerly for her to join him at his place after she would send her children to school. She would look after him, play Scrabble with him, and read him stories. They would go for short trips and visit his family and friends. My *chitthappa* was a regular visitor. Every evening he would drive up to see Appa and spend the evening entertaining him. His sisters also spent quality time with him.

Appa had stopped painting, as he could not stand for long and he could not concentrate. He also had problems seeing with his one eye. His mental canvas was ready. "Moham, I know I will be back on this earth," Appa speculated. They fondly spoke about the day Chandra had gone into a trance and sketched their past lives to them several years ago.

"What animal or person are you going to return to this earth as?" asked Amma.

"Of course, as a man, and I know I want the same wife and the same three daughters," he speculated. "Next time I'll be a better husband and the best father. I promise."

Appa, do not change, as I may fail to recognize you in my next life.

CHAPTER 23
Recovering from Surgery

> Life is an opportunity, benefit from it.
> Life is beauty, admire it.
> Life is bliss, taste it.
> Life is a dream, realize it.
> Life is a challenge, meet it.
> Life is duty, complete it.
> Life is a game, play it.
> Life is a promise, fulfill it.
> Life is sorrow, overcome it.
> Life is a song, sing it.
> Life is a struggle, accept it.
> Life is a tragedy, accept it.
> Life is an adventure, dare it.
> Life is luck, make it.
> Life is too precious, do not destroy it.
> Life is life, fight for it.
> —Mother Teresa

"You can't brood around and be so miserable," said my husband. "We're all upset by your loss, but you can't forget all those who are alive," he said as he gave me a consoling hug. "It's been more than a month and it's time for you to start enjoying your *Appa*'s life."

"I know. I'll be okay. It's just that I wasn't even there. I wonder what happened to Prema, who was there attending to Appa day after day. What did she feel when she saw him take his last breath? My mother was so dependent on Prema during Appa's illness, and you know he wasn't easy to attend to," I reminded my husband.

Appa's dependence on his three daughters could not be quantified. During his illness, Prema and Mother were in charge some of the time, and Appa was in charge most of the time. There were days when he was absolutely normal and could do almost anything, but he would constantly want them at his beck and call. One has to be sick to realize the degree of dependency one wants to exhibit. I was a witness to this when I landed in Mumbai to be with Appa. It was his third day after his major surgery. My flight landed at 4 a.m. and I went to my brother-in-law's home to wash before I went to see Appa. In the meantime, my sister and my mother returned from their harrowing experience of Appa's demanding postoperative care. This was in the famous Tata Cancer Hospital, where Appa was in a private room. My sister and my mother had a bed to lie down in, in the same room. Bad idea! "I want to do something, as I'm bored and I can't take this. I want to go home this minute, as I can't take this place anymore." Even if Appa did not need anything, he kept on grumbling.

"Well, Appa, tomorrow will be a better day," my sister told him testily. "Your daughter from Toronto will be here. She'll keep you entertained and will be energetic and interested in doing things with you. We are this close to leaving you under the mercy of that big nurse who came in to bark at you because you did not take your medication. If you continually whine, we're leaving for Hema's place."

"Well, ask Hema to come," replied Appa. "She's much nicer to me than the two of you put together." Hema, my sister-in-law, was another good soul who gave in to Appa's whims and fancies.

Mom and Prema returned to Hema and Vasan's place, and it was time for me to just ask them briefly about Appa before I took off to see him and take care of him till 5 p.m. Then the shift would change and my poor sister and mother would return to listen to Appa. I hoped to cure him—after all, I am the doctor daughter who knows all about disease and compassion. I was returning to India after six years, and the noise, crowd, traffic, and jet lag created a neural exhaustion that was difficult to comprehend. I was glad to be in Appa's room and sad to see that he did look different after his gruesome experience under the surgeon's knife. Nevertheless, Appa had not lost his soul, personality, or the verve to live. I was quite amazed at his recovery. I must commend those who provided the excellent care that he received at the hospital. His surgeon Dr. Mehta had done an amazing job.

With my jet lag and extreme exhaustion, I was not even sure if I was a capable candidate to take care of anyone after a major surgery. But then, doctors are supposed to be superhuman, and Prema and Mother probably figured that I was well seasoned from on-call and shift work and that this would be a piece of cake. I just had one patient (Appa), not a whole floor under my care.

"Appa, I am so jet lagged that I am not even thinking straight," I said after giving him a hug and asking about his surgery.

"That is okay, *kanna,* my dear," Appa consoled me. "You just relax. There is a bed, and no one will disturb you." I was not surprised at Appa's response, as he had a soft spot for me.

The door opened and the big bully nurse stomped in. She saw me and roared, "Who do we have here? She looks like a close relative. The resemblance is uncanny. She must be the capable doctor from abroad!"

If I was competent and accomplished, I just forgot the definition of capability. She had a list of medications in her hand that were prescribed for Appa, and I did not

Relentless Brush Strokes

know what she wanted me to do. I looked at her and waited for her to continue to bellow.

"Well, my dear doctor from the famous city of Toronto, you can't be sitting around looking pretty. It's time for you to start your duty. The first one happens to be bringing in the medication from the pharmacy. I need for you to go right this instant. The pharmacy is across the way. It's a block from here." She ordered me to run there with her prescription. In Indian hospitals, the patient's family fills the prescription and brings it to the nursing station.

I was so dumbfounded that I couldn't come up with a right answer. My jet-lagged brain took a few seconds to react; or it was the inertia that would not let me find the feet to pitter away to find a pharmacy in this mind-boggling, overcrowded Mumbai. I realized that Toronto had taken away something from me. I didn't know if I could make it even for another day here. Had I ever grown up here? I seemed to be at a loss about how to go about getting this simple job done—bringing in the medicine. Surely, there must be an easier way. I did not have a car, and if I'd tried driving one in the streets of Mumbai, I would have been in another hospital receiving care, or at a police station receiving punishment for careless driving by myself or by somebody else who had hit me because I was in their way.

My father was quick to the rescue. He stood up to the Big Bertha nurse and told her, "She has just arrived from Toronto. First of all, she has jet lag; and secondly, I would not trust her to safely cross the streets. I'm afraid you have to send the peon for my medication."

With an angry twist to her waist, she told my father, "This daughter from Toronto shouldn't be here taking care of you. Here I thought 'foreign trained' meant 'far superior'. You are telling me she needs to be taught to cross the road?!"

I usually have better comebacks, but the neural network was definitely in disarray and I let her go. Appa was overprotective of his poor, incompetent daughter after the insults that she had been subjected to by an unknown woman. He quickly came up to me and said, "You don't worry about anything, my *chellam,* my pet. I am here for you. You need to take some rest and get over this jet lag."

Guess who was taking care of whom at this point? Appa was at his best. My mother and Prema must have been exhausted to even tell me that Appa was a difficult patient. On his fourth postoperative day, he was taking care of his jet-lagged *chellam.* What more did I need? Appa covered me with a blanket and sat next to me for a while. Before I could say jack rabbit, I was in the arms of the sleep fairy. At 1 p.m. Appa woke me up and said my lunch from home had arrived and that I should eat.

"Appa, how did the lunch arrive at the hospital?" I asked.

"The famous Mumbai Dubba Walla was arranged, and he brought it in for you from Hema's home."

Now can you believe this? It was a hot home-cooked meal from my sister-in-law. Her home was almost two hours away from the hospital and the meal was piping hot. They had something for Appa too, but he was not up to it. He ate the hospital food.

"Do you want tea?" Appa asked.

"I can go and get it, Appa. You just have to tell me where the cafeteria is."

"No no! I'll make you fresh tea," Appa said.

"But, Appa, you should be resting. I can surely make my tea. I know how to make it."

"I won't trust you with the stove and the kettle. You've forgotten how to live in Indian circumstances. I can't trust you with a hot stove." There he was busy boiling the water and taking care of his incapable foreign daughter. Big Bertha came in and saw that the medicines had been picked up by the hospital peon. Appa had given him a tip and he'd gone off happily. But I did not escape from Big Bertha's wrath.

"Now that you are up from your beauty sleep, are you ready to take over the duty and look after your father?" she questioned.

"I'm up and I will," I said as I replied with a frog in my throat. She brought on emotions at various levels. First of all, I did not know whether I should feel sorry for my father who had an old goat for a nurse or sorry for myself as she aped me for not knowing the basics of errand running in Mumbai.

Anyway, Appa and I were having a good talk about his surgery and how the procedure was done. Before long, my mother and Prema arrived for their evening duty. The scene changed from an Appa who was capable of taking care of himself and his jet-lagged daughter to a helpless man.

"I think you should not leave Lalitha all alone. With her jet lag, she finds it difficult. Poor girl," Appa related to Mom all that happened in the morning.

Big Bertha walked in and added her few cents. "At last someone who knows how to take care of the sick has arrived." Oh boy!—she had it in for me. I would have failed the rotation as a medical intern at Tata Cancer Hospital if I'd had anything to do with Big Bertha.

It was time for us to return to Madras with Appa and Amma. The four of us boarded a flight and landed in Madras. This was the easiest part of the whole operation of transporting and transplanting ourselves to Appa's home. Their home had been closed up for six months, and it was dusty with a musky odor. The servant who had been serving the family had arrived early in the morning to dust and clean up the place, and she was happy to see that her dear family whom she had been working for had survived the cancer ordeal. She now felt that under her diligent supervision and daily prayers, Appa's cancer would be eradicated. She came up to me and said, "A doctor's job is at a hospital. Your Appa is in better hands now." She meant her hands. "You will see that he will not need any more hospital visits. You can be a daughter and not a doctor," she said consolingly.

The house was not livable. The electricity and water were there, but the telephone service had been temporarily stopped. Amma and Appa had been communicating by telephone and not telegram. "Lalla, you have to go with your sister and pay the dues and get the telephone established for our home," Amma said.

"That's no problem, Amma," I said overconfidently. "It's simple. I'll just go to Prema's house and call the phone company."

"Who are you kidding, Lalla? This is India and not Canada. Here we don't have Bell Canada. You have to personally go and stand in a queue and ask them to resume the connection. It may be a telephone company, but in India they do not answer the phone."

"Okay, Amma. I'll do it right now."

"One more thing you have to remember. You won't get the telephone hooked up unless you're a doctor or some big politician," she warned me. "Please let them know that you are a doctor and they may help you."

"Okay," and I left for Prema's place to pick her up to go to the telephone company. Prema lived a stone's throw away. The reason my parents had their home in Madras was to be close to Prema, where she would be able to attend to them.

The uneven pavement made it difficult to walk. The cows added a hurdle to the walk path. The stray dogs barked at me, as they saw a new stranger in their neighborhood. Despite the fear I had in the pit of my stomach, I somehow made it to my sister's place. Little did I know that there was another drama unfolding. I reached her home and at the bottom of the stairs I was greeted by a territorial canine that had its fangs bared at me. I called out to her and she came up to the balcony.

"Prema, this dog is making it difficult for me to cross over to your place. I'm scared that he'll get a good chunk of flesh from me if I come near your house."

"You have reasons to worry. He's a nasty animal. He just bit my husband and he has left for his rabies shot," she said.

Hearing the commotion, the rightful owner of the dog came to rescue his animal from the two grumbling sisters. "My dog is a very good animal. He won't bite. You can go ahead," he said.

"He's already bitten one member of the family! I don't want him to bite my sister too!" Prema spat at him.

I quickly slithered and dodged from the four-legged mammal, who went on to whimper and whine behind his protective master.

"Seriously, you have to take your dog for some behavior training," I told the owner.

"Your family needs some coaching too, about how to conduct themselves near dogs. These animals can sense dog lovers," he angrily told me off. I didn't think there were any schools to train dogs, or for that matter schools to train humans who encountered neighbors' dogs.

Finally, Prema and I took off to get the telephone issues behind us once and for all. I was not going to make this treacherous trip dodging rabid four-legged man's best friends anymore.

"Prema, Amma told me that this telephone hookup is a simple affair. We just need to go to the office and let them know that there's a sick man who needs medical attention and I'm a doctor."

"Your mother has become a cross between an Indian and American. She has forgotten that this may not fly."

Anyway, I thought that if a smile and a courteous customer couldn't get their telephone line reconnected, then I would say that I had a sick father at home; and if that failed, I would pull out the trump card that I was a doctor and all that jazz, which might do it. But the last resort would be the all-powerful grease that never fails—ten crispy hundred-rupee notes that might get my family's instantaneous communication with the external world reestablished.

I have been to the Bell Canada center in Toronto, and I did not expect a large multistory building in Madras, but with the Indians flying high with computers and communications, I was hoping to see at least a small glass building or at the very least a building with some windows. Wrong! I first thought my sister had lost her way. We were going through a gully that allowed only one person at a time to ascend to God's fortress that blessed homes with telephones. The bully who served us deserves an honorable mention in this memoir. That day, I actually preferred hanging off the fangs of the rabid canine.

"My parents need to rehook their telephone line," Prema said. "They were away for six months and have returned to Madras before their six months was over. Is there any way we can resume our billings for our address?"

"There is a two-month waiting period and we lost some staff and I do not believe that we can do this for another three months," said the bully behind the counter.

"But, my father is sick and we need the telephone, especially if there is an emergency and we need to call a doctor," retorted my sister. The second line of action was failing, as I saw the man mercilessly shaking his head, all entreaties in vain. I saw the urgency to use the third line of action before we resorted to the most extreme measure.

"I am a doctor and I need the telephone for conducting my practice," I implored.

There was a flicker of hope, as I saw the phone man show some interest in my profession.

"What kind of a doctor are you?" he asked with a smug smile, thinking that I was lying.

"I'm a radiologist," and I saw that I was slowly losing my ground. He did not know what a radiologist was and I explained that I read X-rays and CT scans and MRI scans.

His expression changed and I thought that there was some hope after this short course on what my job entailed me to do. "Do you practice at Apollo's hospital?" he asked interestedly.

"I work in Toronto."

As soon as I said that name, it took only milliseconds for the bully to react. "You may be a doctor in Toronto, but how does it matter to me or the Indian Telephone

Company?" Spoken by a man who saw no reason to let this family have their telephone back. My sister glared at me, and I knew that she was mad at my honesty.

"Lalla, why couldn't you just say that you worked at Apollo's? For once, couldn't you have stretched the truth?"

"But, Prema, this is about a *telephone*."

"Lalla, this is about India."

Finally, the two sisters parted with their crisp rupee notes under the table and victoriously emerged from the clasp of the bribing bully.

Now, I did feel that my duties were taking new directions. The servant claimed that she could cure Appa, and if she failed, the telephone was there to make the important calls for cure. We related the story to Amma and Appa, and like children Prema and I enacted the whole scene for their viewing pleasure.

"Lalla, in India, where a job gives a man control over others, he will abuse it to the fullest," Appa said. "His income is half labor and half kickback. Don't you remember our neighbor Kickback Krishnan?" Appa was right. These men who ardently practiced their profession swore a small sum to the temple with a hope of not getting caught.

A year passed, and Appa was slowly sinking. Cancer was taking over his already small frame. The next MRI showed the spread of cancer into his brain and base of his skull. To this date I have not had the heart to pick up the MRI to see the spread of cancer through my father's body. I got a call from Amma that Appa was in a coma after having received chemotherapy. I immediately left for India. As I was on the flight, I was hoping that I would get to see Appa before he passed away. I wanted to say my goodbye to him. I landed in Madras and my brother-in-law came to pick me up at the airport.

Appa had been in a coma for four days.

"Moham, Lalitha is coming today," Appa said. "Could you please let me have my shave? I want a clean *veshti* and the shirt that her husband gave me." Amma was shocked and surprised at the change in my father's mental status. His upgrade from coma to consciousness and awareness of the arrival of his daughter from Toronto was making everyone celebrate. I arrived and was happy to hear that Appa had made it this time. As I walked in, I saw his wasted body and could not help but weep.

My mother took me away from his bed and told me off firmly. "You are here to make him happy. He has woken from his coma just hearing us all speak about you. I will not let you cry in front of Appa." It was hard to see that he was not who I had seen a few months ago. He probably weighed eighty pounds or less. He could barely move. The bed was too hard for his bony frame. The next six weeks I slept next to him. My sister and I played

Scrabble and cards with him. We read funny articles and kept him amused. His eyes needed attention. The tumor had paralyzed his blinking action, and his eye, which was being pushed by the tumor, continually watered and got infected. I would tell Appa that I could clean his eyes and apply the medication.

"No! I want Prema. She is my nurse. She knows how to take care of me."

The six weeks flew by and I knew that this might be the last time that I was going to see my father alive. My heart was heavy and I just could not bid my farewell. It was hard to pry myself away from him.

The Tata Hospital surgeon said that he needed another surgery to remove the tumor.

"I am a happy man," Appa announced, accepting his condition. "I have lived my life. I don't need to suffer and make my family suffer with me. I don't want any surgery."

My sister Swathi visited him immediately after I returned.

"Swathi, how is he doing?" I asked.

"For me, Appa is dead. I cannot bear to see him this way," she told me, crying and describing how he had deteriorated rapidly in the last month.

A month had passed since Swathi returned from Madras. Life was going on as usual and we were going

Relentless Brush Strokes

about doing our duties as if all was okay with Appa. He was constantly on our mind.

I got a message from Hema and Vasan that they had gone to visit Appa. He was frail and did not look good. Amma was not able to take care of him. They told me that Appa was on his way to the hospital.

"Moham and Hema," Appa said. "This will be the last time I will go to the hospital. I can't see myself returning."

"Ennah, you will be alright," Amma consoled him. "Just continue to say your Gayatri mantra."

"Moham, when I am gone, you are going to be all alone. I don't want you to be afraid of anything. Even when someone knocks on the door, you call out loudly, 'Ennah, could you please open the door? I am busy in the kitchen.' This way, anyone, especially strangers, will think that you are not alone and your husband is there to protect you."

"Ennah, you are going to live. Please don't talk like that."

"Moham, you have to face reality. The time has come for me to go. I want you to keep the red dot on. Please don't behave like Indian widows and remove the dot. After all, you are a Hindu, and the significance of putting a dot on our forehead is symbolic of the divine intuitive vision. There are no scriptures that ask for a Hindu to stop wearing this at any time in our lives. This dot is for your protection. Anyone who sees you will assume you have a partner, and harm will not come your way."

I got a phone call from Amma in the morning. Appa had been admitted to Isabella Hospital. My friend who was a doctor and did his residency training with me told my mother that Appa was not going home this time.

"Amma, when do you want me to come?" I asked her.

"It's very hot. I don't want to take care of you and Appa. He's very sick and I think this is it for him."

"Moham, when is Lalitha coming to see me?" Appa asked.

"I have spoken to her today," Amma dodged his question. He repeatedly asked for me during his last few hours of clear thinking. Finally, he told Amma, "Look Moham, Lalitha has come." Amma did not disagree with his hallucination. If he is able to see his daughter in his mind's eye, who is she to dispute with a dying man? Appa looked for the last time at his daughter, as he closed his eyes. "Yes, she is here with you," Amma said.

Appa had his final canvas prepared. He had in his imagination a painting—the arrival of his daughter at his bedside. Who can stop him from doing that? Nobody can.

It was 5 in the evening. I was at home taking care of my daughters and their friend whose mother was away.

Relentless Brush Strokes

"Mom, I found the diamond that Dad lost," my daughter and her friend came running up to me excitedly, showing off the shiny stone that they had found while playing in the front foyer. My husband had had this diamond ring presented to him by Appa. A week ago he had lost the stone from the ring.

Superstitions now raced through my thoughts. Oh my God! It is a bad to omen to lose your diamond, but it is worse to find it. I wish it had stayed lost. I hoped nothing bad happened.

The phone rang. "This is the Isabella Hospital nurse calling from Madras. Your father passed away."

"I want to speak to my mother or my sister, please."

"I'm sorry. They have left the hospital. They've gone to make the funeral arrangements. There is no one from your family here to speak to you."

I just sat down. An impersonal message from a nurse with no sympathy—no tearful sister to tell me everything that happened. Where was my mother when I needed her? Was she not the one who should have called me? Why did they leave me on my own to receive this last message? What a cruel nurse with no sensitivity. She'd done that on purpose—sent my mother and my sister away so she could make this phone call and feel important for a minute. An ego trip for the nurse. Where had they all gone? I wanted to talk to my mother. I wanted to talk to my sister. The funeral must wait. I was far away. I wanted to be there. Didn't they all want me? I tried fruitlessly to reach everyone.

I called my sister Swathi in LA. We wept together. The final varnish of tears was sprayed over my father's imaginary painting. I refused to take phone calls. I did not want to speak to anyone except my mother and my sister. I did not wish to see anyone except my children and my husband. No one could make me feel better. Friends visited me and said that time was the best healer. After fifteen years, the memory of that day can still bring hot tears prickling through my eyes, and my heart feels heavy. I understand that we all have to go. But when it is your parent, you become a child again and forget to act mature when the final goodbye is being said.

Finally, Amma spoke to me. "Lalla, Appa continued to say, 'Om Namo Narayana' and 'Om Namah Shivaya.'" Om = infinity and immortality; Namo = take this name in honor; Nara = man, and ayana = eternity. The chant "Om Namo Narayana" means man's eternal passage through birth, life, and death. *Na* means earth, *mah* water, *shi* fire, *va* wind, and *ya* sky. And the chant "Om Namah Shivaya" means to destroy all negative qualities and bring one to immortality.

"We were all there when he took his last breath," Amma said. "He had the exclusive room where Jesus

Christ on his cross was above the head of his bed, and in the early morning the church bell rang as your *Appa* took his last breath."

Amma, what are you saying? Amma could not control herself, as she told me about all the religious rites that were being performed before Appa was finally taken for cremation. Appa was finally merging religions before he departed this world. Amma did not see the difference between the church bells and the temple bells. She was delighted that Jesus on his cross guided Appa. Appa's close friend Vimal, a Christian who had gone on a sightseeing tour to Benaras, came home with holy water from the Ganges in a sealed copper vessel on the day of the cremation. Finally, Appa, who had told me that it was okay to say the Catholic hymn in front of Hindu idols at home, had his last hour spent under the watchful eyes of Jesus as he chanted his Hindu mantras. Appa had a hero's funeral. All his students, family, and friends were there paying their respect to him. His favorite flowers were showered on him before his final passage into eternity.

CHAPTER 24
Appa's Memories Are Alive

> The tissue of life to be
> We weave with colors all our own
> And in the field of destiny
> We reap as we have sown.
> —John G. Whittier

It is September. Almost four months since Appa passed away. Amma has not been doing well. Her neighbors and friends are up to their eyeballs with her constant lamentations. It had come to the point that her family doctor, Appa's good friend, told Amma that she had to keep herself active and do something else.

"I know you miss him. After all, you were married to him for forty-three years. But mourning like this is not helping you, and he is not going to come back. Your health will suffer. Why don't you go back to teaching at the school?"

For Amma, her home and environment were a continuous reminder of Appa's final days. She relived the suffering and grieved.

"Amma needs to go away from these surroundings, to not remember Appa every waking second of her life." Prema called me up to say that I should bring Amma over to Toronto.

I was not doing very well either. I had guilt that I was not next to Appa when he'd passed away and still had sorrow over losing him. "If only I had done this for Appa" was a thought that kept ravaging through me and made me into a grieving machine. I did not want to talk to anybody about Appa. The only two people that I would relate to about my father were my husband and my sister Swathi. Even those two strong-willed pillars of support were showing signs of giving up on me.

I went down to the basement to brood about Appa in his painting room. There I saw his paintbrushes and some leftover paint drying in a corner, with dust and cobwebs covering the brushes. I took them to the sink and cleaned up the brushes, and every brush reminded me of Appa. My eyes welled with tears as I brought the brushes upstairs and told my children and my husband that I was going for art lessons at the local community school.

I came home, not too happy with my creation. But that night I could not sleep. I imagined all the styles that Appa used, to create his paintings. I got up at 3 a.m., crept down to Appa's painting room, and decided to walk like him around the painting that I was creating.

I came close to the canvas and tossed a little purple mixed with zinc white and cobalt blue. Then I walked far from the painting and imagined what Appa might have done to give contour and to project distance to a far-off mountain. I quickly mixed colors of different values and slapped them onto the canvas—shades of green for the trees, a cactus plant in the forefront, and by 8 a.m. I had completed the painting before I could serve breakfast for the family. My excitement knew no bounds. I brought the painting proudly to the kitchen and left it for the family to see before breakfast got served. I ran excitedly and placed my first call.

"Amma, you will not believe this, but I went to the basement and saw Appa's paints and brushes. I decided to join an evening art course."

"I am happy for you."

"Amma, I think I can paint like Appa."

"Your *Appa* would have been proud of you."

"Amma, you don't seem too confident in my artistic ability."

"No, *chellam,* dear. I'm sure you're good. It's just that I have to see it to believe it. Continue painting. One day you may be able to use the paintbrushes."

Amma mentioned that Appa had not been able to paint, as the vision in one eye had been lost from the spread of cancer. His powers of concentration had not been there, and he had wasted away from the cancer. He could not have even sat up in bed without support. His mental faculties had been sharp most of the time and he had one unfinished painting on the easel. "Moham," he'd said. "I want all of the art supplies and easels and all that I possess to be given to my sister. She is a great artist and will pursue painting. It is no use leaving it here for these daughters of mine. They love art, but I do not think they have it in them to paint."

"I will let your sister know that this is a gift from you."

When Amma came to Toronto, I could not wait to take her to the basement to show her the two canvases I had created in the past few weeks. The rich blue skies, the river flowing through, and mountains in the background were my first attempts at spilling colors on my canvas. Every stroke reminded me of Appa. *Appa, why did I not try to paint when you were alive? You would have been so proud of me. I remember how you proudly introduced your three daughters. You could have added another sentence: "She is just like me, an artist."* It was not meant to be.

"Why couldn't you have done this just once when he was alive?" Amma burst out crying when she saw my painting. "You do mix colors like your *Appa*. I can see him smiling from beyond those mountains." We, the two grieving women, kept comforting each other with Appa's memories.

"Your *Appa*'s spirit must have visited Toronto."

"I think so, Amma."

"He knew that your husband was his big support when it came to painting. He handed over the paintbrushes and colors for you to relax and enjoy a hobby that you will cherish." Amma wiped her tears and happily went around our home looking at Appa's creations. She was finally recovering. She had found a place where Appa's spirit was alive, and she had a different task at hand: to console her grieving child who had lost her father recently.

Amma now lives with Appa's spirit in Toronto. We discuss his quirkiness and bring a smile to everyone. We understand that some of his eccentric mannerisms may have raised eyebrows, but his family cherishes every moment we spent with him. Every morning Amma comes down the stairs and walks up to the sunrise scene painted by her husband with her hands folded in prayer position. She knows that Appa and his spirit are alive in his paintings. Appa had dared to dream, and Amma had cultivated his creativity.

GLOSSARY OF TERMS

amma: mother
angavastram: body clothing (literal translation)
appa: father
athai: father's sister
Bhaghavan: God
bidi: tobacco leaves rolled before smoking
Bollywood: a word coined to describe movies made in India
Carnatic: classical music from South India
chitthappa: father's younger brother or mother's younger sister's husband
dowry: cash and kind given by the bride's family to the groom
jubba: a loose-fitting cotton shirt worn by children
kadankaaran: a man living on borrowed time
Kanyadhanam: giving away the bride
karma: action-based destiny
Kashi yaathrai: Benaras travels
kolam: a design made with rice powder to decorate the

front of a family home
Madrasi: a person hailing from Madras
maapillai: bridegroom
Maapillai azhaippu: inviting the bridegroom
Mahabharata: a mythology written several thousand years ago
mandap or *mandapam*: canopy under which a wedding takes place
mantara: (soul freedom) chanting
moksha: liberation from the cycle of death and rebirth
naadhaswaram: a horn or other wind instrument played in the temple and at weddings
namaskaram: respectful folding of hands before another person
paavadai: a long skirt
panchagachcham: the *veshti* wrapped in between the legs
patti: grandmother
payasam or *kheer*: a dessert made from milk to celebrate
Penn parkkum padalam: seeing the girl or future bride
periappa: father's older brother or mother's older sister's husband
poojai: religious prayer
poonal: a sacred white thread worn by Hindu men
prasaadam: an offering to God
puniyav janam: auspicious birth
saastrigal: priest

Sandhyavandanam: prayers done once or twice during the day by men
sanyaasi: a yogi or hermit
Sahasranamam: a hymn in praise of the lord
sloghaas: mantra chanting
Swayamvara: a woman chooses her husband from several suitable men
veshti: material worn around the waist by men; called by some a loin cloth
vibhuthi: ashes
thali: a yellow thread, or black beads worn by married women
thatha: grandfather
thooli: a cloth hamper hung from the ceiling of a room where a child sleeps
varan: a suitable bride or groom
yaar: friend

ACKNOWLEDGMENT

This book is dedicated to my mother. She assisted me with this writing. Her motivation and spiritual encouragement by reading through the script gave me energy to complete this work. She reminded me of some of the anecdotes that I had forgotten. She has been a pillar of support and believed in my writing. She always told me that if you have nothing nice to say about someone, then do not utter any words. In this instance, Appa is not here to defend himself. So, Appa, I hope that I have done justice in my biography of you. This biography just highlights some of my father's spirited ways. My cherished and supportive times with my sisters and my mother made us appreciate all of Appa's eccentricities.

My sisters have always been there through thick and thin, and I was pleasantly surprised by the way I got supportive notes from my cousins Padma, Cheenu, Chandru, and Janani, and my uncles Ramu Mama and Paddu Mama. Paddu Mama reminded me of Appa's involvement in chess games and contract bridge at the local club. Appa had spent several weeks with Paddu Mama and his wife, Nalini, while he was completing the electricity project for the town of Dhanbad when he was an electrical engineer. He hooked up the radio, tape recorder, and gramophone onto one system in the sixties, and it worked. That was never the story in our home, where nothing worked if Appa had meddled with the radio, water heater, or the electrical system. He took his time to complete home projects, as there was no one pushing him to finish it. They have all known my father and enjoyed the anecdotes that I have written.

My brother-in-law, N. V. S. Mani, and his wife, Leela, and Ram and his wife, Stephanie, wrote to me that it was like watching a movie where you knew the stars. They came to know my parents after I got married to their brother. I valued their opinion, as they were like my new parents at my in-laws.

My friends Jillu and Rangan read through some of the chapters and gave me positive feedbacks. My niece Swetha, who had been with her grandfather throughout his grueling fight with cancer read through the story with tears in her eyes. She needs more than just a thank you note. She and her brother Kumar showed compassion, care, and love to their grandparents and were always there to assist them. Many grandchildren need to take lessons from them. Appa's other grandchildren, who were too young, showed respect, care, and sensitivity through their *thatha*'s difficult days. I know for sure that these grandchildren, headed by Swetha, can set up a seniors abode, where love will be the ingredient in the soup that is served and sensitivity the flavor for all days. Most of all, I thank my husband and my children, who have tolerated my mood swings during this painful process of remembering some of the difficult days that Appa went through during his sickness. I owe this book to all of you. My daughters, Samantha and Meghana, helped me with a few of the chapters. Meghana commented, "Who is going to read this? Are you not wasting your time?" I defended my position, "I am doing this for the future generation who may want to know about their family. I know it is not going to be on the New York Times best-seller list."

Appa had two dear students who were at his bedside till he took his last breath. These two teenagers, Sumukhi and Sharadh, have changed the way we all look at teenagers. They were selfless and eager to assist Amma with all their help during some dire circumstances.

My friend Dr. Jitender Sehgal did the photograph for the front cover. He is an excellent photographer, and I cannot thank him enough.

Last but not the least I am forever indebted to Author House, Ingram Publishers, Brian Mattox, Jeremiah Murphy, and Katie Schneider, and all of the support staff at the publishers who have provided thoughtful correction with their experience and keen eyes while editing the book.

ABOUT THE AUTHOR

Dr. Lalitha Shankar was born in India. She lives in Toronto with her husband and two children. She is a practising physician in Toronto. She received the "Professional women of the Year Award" from ICCC in 2002. She is a coauthor of several medical books, but this is her first non-medical book. The sales proceeds from this book is being donated to the charity: Handicare International, a registered Canadian Charity based in Toronto, Canada.(www.handicareintl.org)

Printed in the United States
12732818LV00001B/304-375/P